A JOURNEY of BODY & SOUL

a memoir

TRACH BA VU

RIVER GROVE
BOOKS

NOTE: Throughout this book, medical patients' names have been changed to protect confidentiality.

Published by River Grove Books
Austin, TX
www.greenleafbookgroup.com

Copyright ©2013 Trach Ba Vu

All rights reserved.

No part of this book may be reproduced, stored in a retrieval system, or transmitted by any means, electronic, mechanical, photocopying, recording, or otherwise, without written permission from the copyright holder.

Design and composition by Greenleaf Book Group LLC
Cover design by Greenleaf Book Group LLC
Cover credits: ©iStockphoto.com/track5; ©iStockphoto.com/Bim

Publisher's Cataloging-In-Publication Data
Vu, Trach Ba.
  A journey of body & soul : a memoir / Trach Ba Vu. -- 1st ed.
    p. ; cm.
  Issued also as an ebook.
  ISBN: 978-1-938416-43-9 (hardcover)
  ISBN: 978-1-938416-53-8 (pbk.)

    1. Vu, Anna. 2. Vietnamese American women--Biography. 3. Women physicians--United States--Biography. 4. Vietnamese Americans--Social conditions. 5. Spiritual life. 6. Biography. I. Title. II. Title: Journey of body and soul
E184.V53 V8 2013
973/.004959/22092   2013950004

First Edition

I dedicate this book to my children: Linh, Daryl, Anna, David, Trien, Andrea, Hoang, Thuy, Triet, Shera, Jerome, and Julie, and also especially to my wife, Lan Vu. I accomplished this because of their confidence, love, and pride in me.

CONTENTS

Preface vii
1. Journey into the World 1
2. Unpredictable Journey 19
3. Journeys of Remorse, Journeys of Healing 49
4. Journey to the Past 79
5. A Journey of Spiritual Encounters 115
6. Journeys into Mystery, Love, and Divinity 131
7. Back to the Lonely Journey 187
8. Journey to Destiny 239
Acknowledgments 275
About the Author 277

PREFACE

This is the true story of a girl who was born in a faraway country where there was no peace for thousands of years. She came into this world during a war that was unpopular, costly, and humiliating to many: the Vietnam War. This war brought her to the United States of America at the age of eight and a half years. Being born in the war and living constantly in danger, she had to mature faster than other children her age.

From her first day in school, even though living in difficult situations, she dreamed of becoming a medical doctor. The seed of her career, as she later believed, was passed down generation to generation from her distant ancestors.

Coming to a new country and facing the obstacles of a strange culture, new ways of life, a foreign environment, and especially an unfamiliar language, she thought at first her dream had been shattered. Gradually, with a strong will and courage from her family, she regained her confidence and continued to pursue her goals.

Having witnessed many deaths by an early age, she never forgot what she had seen. She wondered why there were wars and what happened to people after they died. Born and raised in a devout Catholic home, she never had any doubt of what was taught by the Church until personal experiences led her to question the Church's teachings. Extraordinary phenomena that could not be explained nor supported by the Church propelled her more and more into a determined investigation of the issue of life after death.

As she pursued her education in the United States, memories of the war continued to haunt and torture her with nightmares. Though she went to great effort to forget, the terrible images of violence would not leave her in peace. Conflicting interpretations of the war confused her. What she learned and heard from US history books and her teachers was in great contrast to what her parents and their friends told her. She had thought of the Vietnam War as a holy cause that involved several generations of her family, both maternal and paternal. She vowed to find out the truth of the war whenever she had an opportunity.

Leaving the war-torn country of Vietnam to live and grow up in the peaceful United States of America, she successfully reached her goal to be a physician, but she failed to find personal happiness, trapped as she was between two cultures. In her journey to know the destiny of the human soul, she was caught between her religious beliefs and the supernatural phenomena she encountered. Uncertain what to believe in, she encountered opposition from various churches arising from the matter of her divorce. Still, because of her spiritual confusion and the differing teachings she had experienced, she did not realize that even her father considered divorce a shame to the family until it was too late. And yet, for good or ill, she was determined to find love. For Anna, love ended in pain and loss; pain led her deeper onto her spiritual path and her quest for answers about life after death. But finally, love found her on the journey into healing and gave her the meaning she had sought all her life.

CHAPTER 1
JOURNEY INTO THE WORLD

I

It began in a small country between China and India, a tiny nation compared to these two giants. The people of this country had lived with wars for several centuries, either fighting for their independence or with each other. As with other small countries, the lives of this nation's people were mostly at the mercy of the most powerful nations. This small country was unknown to almost everyone until one special war—called the Vietnam War, a war that nobody enjoys talking about.

This war was neither civil nor patriotic. It was the war between two ideologies, communism and democracy, both of which the Vietnamese people were pushed into. Living in this country during this war, one had to fight either for one side or the other; there was no place between. On either side, most men were busy killing the enemy and their compatriots, leaving their wives to take care of themselves and raise their kids at home.

One rainy, dark evening, inside an apartment at a naval barracks in a small town deep in the southernmost part of South Vietnam, a pregnant woman, Lan Vu, began experiencing contractions. She looked worriedly at her nineteen-month-old daughter sleeping on the bunk bed and wondered who would be taking care of this child when she had to go to the hospital. She wished her husband, Trach Vu, a naval lieutenant, were at home at this very moment. He had been away in a joint operation for more than a week, and no one knew when the operation would end.

In the darkness outside, rain poured down. The war was raging, and the sound of gunfire and explosions seemed much closer tonight. Her husband said he was in this war to defend the freedom of South Vietnam. He was away most of the time, but never did she complain about being left alone at home. Tonight, however, was different. She felt so lonely and wished there were no war so that her husband would be with her at the moment of her baby's delivery. As the contractions came stronger and more frequently, she hurried to her neighbor's door, knocking and asking the lady who answered to take in her sleeping daughter. She went back to her room, grabbed the necessities that she had prepared, then walked into the night.

At the gate of the barracks, the guard realized her situation. It was close to curfew, but he hurriedly summoned someone to take her in the sentry's vehicle to the hospital, about a half mile away.

Inside the waiting room of a military hospital, there were nine other expectant ladies without their husbands with them, in line and waiting for their names to be called. Their men might be away at a battle, as her husband was. She remembered how many times he had been close to death: missed by a sniper's bullet four times, mines exploding next to his boat three times, five or six ambushes and attacks when patrolling, and many other times of exchanged fire with the enemy along the riverbanks. Amid the pain of her labor, she silently prayed for her husband's return and for her smooth delivery. She knew there had been many times when wives were expecting their husbands' return to see their newborn children—but the fathers never came. After praying, she tried to remember what she had to do in case her husband's life was sacrificed to the war. She recalled that each time, before going out for the dangerous operation, he never forgot to repeat again and again that his soul would be with her and their children if he got killed. She felt a jolt of fear and loneliness, and tears silently fell from her eyes.

Her fear was precisely justified, because at that very moment the task force of riverboats on which her husband served was under attack. The mission of the task force was to patrol a section of a narrow river to protect a group of salvage workers who were retrieving a naval boat sunk by guerillas. It had been planned as a thirty-hour job, but a strong current and limited space to maneuver made it hard to bring the boat up from deep water. Both sides of the riverbanks were covered with dense foliage, and when the tide ebbed, the boats of the naval task force were fifteen feet below the banks. Crawling in to dig holes behind the thick bushes along the banks, the enemy waited for the lowest tide to launch a daring attack during the first night of the operation.

Having the advantage of high ground, the attackers shot at every boat, instantly killing four crew members and wounding five more.

At the very first moment of gunfire, the left side of the man on Trach Vu's right was shredded into gore and splintered bone. The surviving crew members returned fire with sidearms and machine guns, but the enemy withdrew only after a counterattacking group went ashore, fought with them on land, and chased them away.

2

It was at the exact moment of the enemy attack that the little girl was born. It was in October of 1966 at Can Tho in what was then known as South Vietnam. She came into this world two hours and fifteen minutes after the curfew time. She arrived on the earth as a replacement for the man standing next to her father, who at that same instant had his entire heart obliterated by a blast from a B-57 bomber. Her father only had a light wound on his right leg and returned home four days later. She was born during the highest peak of the war and was given the baptized name Anna, along with her family name, Vu.

The Vu family had come from a small village in North Vietnam situated in rich, alluvial soil carried south by the Red River from China during centuries of rainy seasons. The Vu clan must have lived very close to the coastal area of the southern part of North Vietnam where many European Christian missionaries landed as early as 1503. Most of them were from Spain, passing through to the Philippines.

No one knows how the two groups understood one another during the first contacts. What kind of communication did they use that enabled thousands of Vietnamese to be converted to Christianity during the early days of the sixteenth century? Most of those converted were poor peasants or fishermen, and the members of the Vu clan would be among the earliest converted. Before the European missionaries' arrival, the foundations of Vietnamese culture and value had been built upon the model of China. Religions and philosophies from China dating from 500 BC were introduced into Vietnam during the second century AD, but Buddhism was the dominant religion by the seventh century, during the Ly dynasty. It came to South Vietnam through Thailand, Cambodia, and Laos six centuries later, when the Vietnamese kingdoms expanded into the south.

Until the sixteenth century, Buddhism, Taoism, Confucianism, and ancestor worship were prevalent. Some of these were not really religions but political philosophies, such as Confucianism, which set up a desired social order for a monarchial society. All religions in Vietnam at the time, though different in name, had many things in common. The majority of Vietnamese people were ancestor worshippers. They generally did not understand the concepts of the various religions, but only followed the rituals that were passed down from generation to generation.

Christianity brought to Vietnam a completely different way of life and of worshipping God. The new faith spread and flourished, which threatened the rulers of Vietnam, who believed that they were actual sons of heaven sent to this world to rule people. Anything that elevated the people's worship to something other than the rulers was seen as a threat against heaven. Christianity taught its followers that the only son of God was Jesus Christ, he alone and no one else, and the kings and their court would not tolerate that. Neither could they accept the fact that their citizens abandoned the traditional religions to acquire a new foreign belief.

During the sixteenth century, the number of Christians was considered small enough to not pose a real threat to the regime at the time. However, there were persecutions of Christians on and off during the seventeenth century and following the first half of the eighteenth century. These persecutions were not severe because the country was experiencing a great turmoil among factions vying for rule. Each regime was trying to consolidate support around itself and was less concerned about the growth of this new faith. It was not until the second half of the eighteenth century that persecution became severe. Ministers and Christians were accused of being associated with the king's enemies.

The king decreed that all ministers and Christians be arrested and incarcerated. Detainees were brought to a trial presided over by a local mandarin. Each Christian was led to a crucifix placed on the ground in front of him. Those who openly walked over the crucifix and renounced Christianity were released immediately. Those who refused to do so were executed. The executions were conducted during the night. Each Christian was dropped into the sea with a big, heavy stone hanging from his or her neck.

It was during this time that the Vu clan faced the persecution. Most of the Vu family's members were captured and killed. By the mysterious disposition of fate and thanks to the protection of a knowledge of medicine, one man escaped and enabled the Vu line to continue on to the present. The Vu family remained devout Christians, and in honor of their ancestor, medical careers and Christianity were encouraged in each generation after that. After surviving persecution, the Vu clan chose to live peacefully and happily in the lovely village that it planned to call home for all time. However, the family would be uprooted and carried away by even more historic events and wars.

The French began colonizing Vietnam in 1858, but the Vietnamese people staged many uprisings in the effort to claim their independence. For more than eighty years they resisted foreign rule, until World War II, when most Vu family members volunteered with Ho Chi Minh to fight for the independence of the country.

Anna's grandfather, Chan Vu, was among the first of those who rushed after Ho Chi Minh to fight for independence. He was also one of the first to discover that Ho Chi Minh was a pawn of the communist Soviets, who only used Vietnamese independence as a means toward communism's goal of conquering the whole of Southeast Asia.

Chan Vu abandoned Ho Chi Minh and secretly joined in an anticommunist group in the area but was soon discovered. He was arrested and imprisoned five different times. After his final release and escape to the French quarter of Nam Dinh, the town where he lived, he left some important papers at the village church inside a statue. He took his family to South Vietnam in 1954 to avoid the communist regime. Here his son, Anna's father, met and married Anna's mother.

The story of Anna's mother's family is completely different. Anna's maternal grandfather, a teacher and also a nurse, was originally an atheist. His belief was that death ends everything: no soul, no God, neither heaven nor hell. His wife, Anna's grandmother, was a Buddhist. After they met and became engaged, she fell into a kind of mental illness. As a nurse, he came to take care of her very often.

One day, when talking to him, she suddenly stopped, stared in the direction of the gate, and uttered aloud, "We have company. A strange man, a European, is coming."

"Who is coming?" he asked, looking in the direction she was pointing and seeing no one. "There is nobody coming."

"It is not a strange man. He is Jesus Christ," she said.

She then knelt down silently at the door with her eyes rolling up in her head and her hands clasped under her chin. After about two minutes she regained consciousness and told him, "Jesus already left. Before leaving, he promised to come back in five days to take me on a tour." She was surly and angry when perceiving that he seemed not to believe one word of what she had said.

Though he didn't believe her seemingly weird and demented words, he came five days later to see what would happen. What he witnessed that day would change his faith completely. His fiancée had woken early and was busy preparing for the appointment with Jesus. She took a shower, put on all white clothes, and at the indicated time, lay face up on the bed, her arms along her body and her legs straight. A wet handkerchief covered her eyes; she looked like a corpse on a gurney. Presently, as he watched, her heartbeat stopped. About ten minutes later, her body was gently raised up from the bed and lowered to the ground. He placed her on the bed again.

In some minutes, she woke up and looked around, puzzled. She then smiled at him and announced, "Sir, I am not your fiancée. I am a female saint that God sent to protect the body of your friend from disturbance by devils." She then walked around the house, like a visitor who wanted to see what the house looked like. Then she lay down in the same position as previously and stayed completely immobile.

He sat waiting anxiously without knowing what to do.

About four hours later, she woke up again and, speaking in the tone of his fiancée, began narrating her "tour."

"First, Jesus immersed my soul in a well to clean me from any vestige of sin. After cleaning, I became light and floated high on the sky, flying after him all around the world."

She then cited the names and described the details of each place she was brought to. She had sensed the heat of the sun when she and Jesus came close to it. She had been in Africa, Asia, and Europe. On the way back she was foretold of her future poor and short life of drudgery, the number of children she would have, and even her age at her death.

After mulling over these experiences of his fiancée, he abandoned atheism and became a devout Catholic. His fiancée was baptized as a Catholic, her sickness was cured, and they were married and had a dozen children together. Anna's mother was their second daughter; she has five brothers and six sisters.

Through these circumstances, the wars in Vietnam brought a longtime Christian family, the Vus, from North Vietnam to meet the newly Catholic one, the Nguyens, in the South. This was how the marriage of Anna's parents came about. They met and built up a Christian family in which children were born during different times and wars. Anna's father was born at the onset of World War II, her mother at the peak of that war, and Anna at the peak of another one, the Vietnam War. Together, her parents lived almost their whole lives in various wars while raising Anna and her siblings.

3

About two months after Anna's baptism, the war came closer and closer to the residence, and their city was frequently hit by missiles and artillery fire from the enemy. Her father decided to send her mother, Anna, and her older sister to Saigon to live with her paternal grandparents, where she stayed for about five years. Anna's grandparents were very traditional and, probably because they had lived almost constantly in war, they were also very religious. Her grandmother strongly believed in the power of prayers. She asked Anna to pray to God and the Virgin Mary every night before bedtime for the safety of each member of the family, especially for her father.

Two brothers came after Anna, born between 1968 and 1970 During this period, they all lived together: grandparents, mother, and four children. Anna was very close to her grandma. Sharing the same room, her grandma often massaged and scratched Anna's back and lulled her into sleep with religious stories. Anna was very scared of the dark when being left alone even though her grandma assured her that there was no such thing as a ghost. She told Anna that devils came from hell, pretending to be ghosts to weaken her faith, but she assured Anna that when a person dies, the soul would either go straight to heaven if righteous, to purgatory if some light sins were committed, or to hell if guilty of grave sins. No soul was permitted to wander around the earth, she told Anna.

Anna and her sister were sent to Catholic school to strengthen their faith, to prepare for their first confession, and most of all to learn that they were born with sins: original sin and everyday sin. That's why when beginning her prayers, Anna always started with the words, "Oh God, I am a sinner...."

At school, Anna had two close friends, Cynthia and Sandra. They shared whatever each had brought from home: candies, toys, fruits, and some funny stories. Cynthia was very good in mathematics and dreamed of becoming a math teacher. Sandra hoped to be a pharmacist like her aunt, her mother's sister. Anna knew she wanted to be a medical doctor, but she did not want to tell anyone. Once when her mother asked what she wanted to become, Anna told her mother, "Probably a nun like Sister Cecilia," a teacher at school. Her mother knew Anna was only kidding but decided not to push for the real answer, thinking that Anna was too young to know.

One year, a month before summer vacation, Cynthia dropped out of school. She did not say a word to her two best friends about why she quit, nor did their teacher know why. Anna and Sandra missed her and wished her back. Much later, Sister Cecilia revealed that Cynthia's father had been killed in a fierce battle in the central highlands of Vietnam. Cynthia's mother took her children back to their native city, where they couldn't go to school at all. There were many students who experienced this same misfortune during Anna's school years and Sandra and Anna knew the same thing could happen to them, too.

Following the Tet Offensive of 1968, the daring but suicidal failed attack of the North Vietnamese Army and the Viet Cong who hoped to overthrow South Vietnam's government, there was a temporary, peaceful lull in Saigon. During this time, Anna's father was stationed in several places. Finally, though, in 1973, he was assigned to a stable position in Da Nang, one of the northernmost cities of South Vietnam. For economic reasons, Anna's mother decided to move with her children to be with her husband. Anna did not want to move, but she had to. It was her turn to leave school, memories, and friends behind, with little hope of seeing them again.

4

Anna's mother leased a flat to open a new business, a bookstore that she hoped would help support the family. Her business went well for about fourteen months, but then the North Vietnamese communists began a full advance to invade the South again.

Being cut off from all war supplies from the United States, South Vietnam was ill prepared to push back the enemy, who maintained full support from the Communist Bloc. The defense forces of South Vietnam withdrew from one city after the other, including where Anna's family resided. Remembering past experiences of communist atrocity, thousands and thousands of old people, women, and children hit the roads, carrying what they could and trying to head south. Refugees filled every corner of the cities and caused severe traffic jams. Roads to the hoped-for escape routes were full. The airports were jammed. Aircraft could not take off or land because of refugees on the runways. Thousands of civilians went to naval bases or the beaches, looking for ships or boats to take them out of the country.

The communists pursued with mortars, artillery, and missiles. Many civilians and soldiers got killed on the roads and were ignored and pushed aside by runaway people. There was no room for mercy.

A mortar round struck next to Anna's house, downing electric lines that tumbled onto the fiber roof of her house. Sparks showered down and the electricity popped and fizzed loudly; everyone was terrified and ran outside. On the street in front of her house, people rushed back and forth, looking for their lost children. Gunfire came closer every moment. Anna's mother was desperately looking for the means to take her children away. At last, Anna's father sent transportation just in time to take them into the base before the arrival of the enemy's tanks. Her mother left behind everything she had built up and ran for her life and the lives of her children.

Many civilian families were not as lucky as Anna's. Of the thousands of people who rushed to the naval base or the beach nearby, only a few were allowed to board the small barges pulled by motorboats. There was no food or water for the escapees, and many children died on the way to safer places.

Once aboard an escape ship, Anna's mother wept quietly. She worried about how she and her children would survive without money. She had left behind all her frugal savings, everything she had worked so hard for; it was all gone. She looked at her children with fear in her heart. Now she was alone again; what might happen to her husband, still left behind? Would he get out safely? If he didn't, then how would she manage to raise four children? What would become of South Vietnam? Would her family be safe in the south? Her mother's mood made Anna cry, too. Like her siblings, she was very young to be living through such an anguishing experience.

While Anna, her mother, and her sister and brothers were safely on their way to the south, her father stayed behind and fought with his unit until the last moment, until the whole naval base was crushed. Left behind by the navy as the base fell to the communists, he ran to the beach and was unable to find transportation to get out. He was rescued at last by a navy officer whose boat happened to pass by.

Two days later, he found what remained of his unit, taking refuge at another naval base at the coastal city of Cat Lo, eighty miles east of the capital. His wife and children were back at his parents' house by this time. After fifteen days of hard duty at the new location,

Anna's father took some days of leave to check on his family in the capital. The road back to his new base was cut off by the enemy after just one day with his family, and when he requested transportation to return to duty, his headquarters in Saigon told him only to wait. He returned to his wife and children, at a loss for what to do as the bad news from the war kept coming, getting worse and worse.

5

The situation of South Vietnam got worse after the resignation of President Nguyen Van Thieu and his replacement by his vice president, Tran Van Huong. Everyone hoped that the new president could negotiate with the other side to bring peace to the rest of the nation, but the communist regime from the North refused to discuss peace, and its conquering force kept advancing. The South bravely fought back, but being short of weapons and supplies, it continued to retreat toward the capital. The US embassy began evacuation of its citizens and those who were working for the US government in Vietnam. Many high-ranking officials, military as well as civilian, had abandoned their posts. The situation was desperate.

The communists were coming, and the same situation of twenty-eight days before in central Vietnam would likely repeat again: evacuation from the capital and the collapse of the South Vietnamese government.

Though still very young, Anna worried and imagined the hardship under the new regime: her father could be killed or thrown in jail. She wondered how her family would survive, because her mother had lost almost everything during the last evacuation. What would her mother do to feed her children? And would she and her brothers and sister be allowed to go to school, or would they be sent to labor in the fields? Anna asked her grandma what she could do and was told to pray for God's help. In her young head, she knew that praying could not stop the enemies from coming, but still she prayed and hoped that God would protect the family one way or another.

The war front came closer and closer, and the capital was besieged. Communists launched more heavy missiles deep into the city to evoke terror and to kill. Again-frightened people were running to the naval ports, airports, or the US embassy, seeking means to escape.

Being cut off from his own unit, Anna's father had no one to ask about the situation or what he should do at the moment. He wanted to take his family away, but how and where? He was hopeless and thought that he either would be killed or would kill himself when the enemy came. Desperately, on an afternoon two days before the end of April 1975, he called his two brothers.

"Communists are going to come," he told them. "Bring something to eat, for I think this will be our last gathering. Once the enemies come, either we will be killed or jailed and then executed. This will be our Last Supper." They drank and ate, ignoring the sounds of artillery and explosions. He hugged his brothers in a gesture of farewell and lay down to sleep on the sofa.

Anna's mother was unable to eat or sleep. In her room, she was greatly troubled by fear. She knew that danger was nearby. She went to her husband and woke him up, saying, "Please do not sleep. Wake up to find means to get out of here. Our family is in terrible danger. Go to naval headquarters to find out what is going on; maybe you can find a way out."

He ignored her warning. She went to him a second time, just ten minutes later, and repeated her plea. He got up, got dressed, and carried his wife on a motorcycle to the naval base. They stopped by the house of a ship's captain. The captain was not home, but his wife told them that her husband had said that all naval ships would depart from the base in thirty minutes, and she did not know the ships' destination.

Anna's parents hurried back home. Her grandfather was waiting for them at the door. Anna's father said to him, "Dad, I have to go; they will kill me if they get me. As for you, you may be killed on the way out if you choose to go with me. You may survive if you stay."

Anna's grandfather replied that he preferred to die on the way out rather than to live with communists.

Anna's father then gathered his family, grabbed what possessions he could, and along with his parents, brothers, wife, and children, rushed to the naval compound. Just as they entered the gate of the base, two enemy airplanes dropped bombs at the airport and its surroundings. Anna and her siblings fell to the ground, terrified of the gunfire and explosions everywhere. Her father had to pick up his shaking children and bring them to the shelter. The curfew was set and no one was permitted to leave the compound.

The whole family took refuge inside the shelter and waited. A few minutes before midnight, the commander-in-chief and high-ranking officers of the navy secretly boarded ship and departed the country. Amid confusion and worries, Anna's father hurriedly collected the family and sought transportation to get out. Along with many other refugees, Anna's family was allowed to go aboard a ship that sailed from the port on the orders of its captain, without any order from higher authorities. All its running lights doused, the ship sailed in darkness away from beleaguered Saigon, ablaze from the continuous mortar and missile attacks of the coming enemy. Every now and then along the way, flares from the outposts alongside the river popped up into the sky as if to say farewell to the ship.

Sadness overwhelmed Anna's father when he thought of the soldiers inside those outposts. They were ignorant of what was going on, faithfully staying on guard at the position assigned to them so that others, including him, could safely get away. He looked back in the direction of Saigon and watched as explosions continuously flared up into the sky. Thousands of soldiers were fighting the enemy as their superior officers deserted them. Many brave men died that night to defend the capital, but no one could count the bodies.

The ship reached the sea safely at dawn. Anna's father did not know where the ship was bound. Surveying the situation, he knew there was no hope to return to Vietnam. At first he thought the commanders of the South Vietnamese forces could regroup and fortify to fight back, yet at the moment, it seemed unlikely to happen that way at all. South Vietnam was indeed collapsing, and so were he and other people like him. He never thought that he and his family would go to the United States, because he believed the US government had betrayed and abandoned Vietnam.

The ship captain communicated with his superiors and was ordered to wait at an assigned location. After the announcement of surrender of the new president, all the South Vietnamese naval ships were on line, heading to the Philippine Islands.

With this news, Anna's father knew that he was leaving the homeland that many generations of his clan had fought to make free. He realized he was no longer a soldier, but a refugee. His whole family had become refugees as well. He looked back with sorrow at the horizon where his country burned, slowly disappearing in the distance, blurred through his tears. For the second time in his life—at the age of thirty-six—he had become a refugee.

When he turned around, Anna was standing quietly about ten feet behind him. He told her, perhaps speaking to himself at the same time, "We have lost everything, including our country."

Anna asked him where the ship was going, but his only answer was a shake of the head. The thought of going to the United States was hateful to him. But the war and fate, not his intentions or thought, were bringing him and his family to a place he disliked.

CHAPTER 2
UNPREDICTABLE JOURNEY

1

Four months later, under the sponsorship of Saint Joseph Medical Center, Anna and her family settled in Wichita, Kansas, after a long and aimless journey. Coming to the mainland United States, instead of staying on Guam as her father had planned, would be a fateful destination for her. They had reached the island territory of Guam not long before the monsoon season. The refugees found themselves in a hurried process that moved them to temporary camps set up in the United States, where they would wait for a sponsorship that would allow them to settle in the United States or any other country in the world willing to accept them. Burning with nostalgia for his native country and anger at the betrayal of the United States and worried about the prejudice and cold weather he might encounter in America, Anna's father was at first determined to stay in Guam. He applied and was approved to settle on this island. Soon, his name was called to bring his family members to a station where a bus would come to pick them. It took too much time to assemble everyone he wanted to go with him, and when he brought them to the indicated place, it was too late; the bus had gone. No one at the settlement office knew when the next bus would come. He brought everyone back to the tent in which they were living and changed his mind about staying in Guam. The next day he filed the paperwork for a request to go to the United States.

Though welcomed to this new land, Anna's parents did not see Wichita, Kansas, as their home or the United States as their country. They were tormented by the memories and humiliation of persons who had been driven out of their homeland. Coming to this country with empty hands and a future full of uncertainties made them worried and depressed. But they had to raise their children and give them hope for their life. They knew they must fight again to survive.

As opposed to her parents, Anna and her siblings did not have deep roots in Vietnam. Anna was born in one place and brought away only one month later. She had followed her father wherever he was posted. Most memories from her early years in Vietnam were of death, sickness, and wounds inflicted by the war: terror from exploding missiles, mines, and bombs. All of these would haunt her for many years to come.

Now, at another strange place, she was enrolled in the fourth grade at an elementary school. She was eight at the time, but since she had enrolled in school in Vietnam at a much younger age than was possible in the United States, she had already completed third grade.

It was frightening for Anna to walk into school on the first day.

Everyone seemed to be staring at her and saying things that she did not understand. Some seemed friendly, but others looked distant and hostile. For several days, all through her classes, she just sat still, made no noise, and tried to imitate what the neighbor students were doing. There was no communication between her and her teacher or with her classmates, because she had never learned one word of English.

Anna and her two other siblings were the only Asian students in this school. Students asked her so many questions that she did not understand. The same questions were asked by different students again and again for several days until Anna could remember how to repeat them herself. From her father, she knew that the students at school were curious about her because she was different. They wanted to know her name, where she came from, and why she had come to the United States.

Unable to answer or explain anything made her uneasy and withdrawn at school. She wanted to tell them that she and the family did not wish to come to the United States but that the war had brought her here; she wanted very much to tell them that she wanted to go back to Vietnam. Living here, she considered herself deaf, mute, and ignorant being unable to speak, hear, or understand anything. She knew only that she and the whole family came to this country because of a war that she did not know anything about. Why were her grandfather and father involved in the war? What had the American government hoped to achieve from the war? Why did the war take place in Vietnam instead of some other country? These were the first concerns of her life. She promised herself that she would find all the answers as soon as she could.

Being unfamiliar with the new environment and atmosphere,

she and her siblings did not make much progress in communication, much less in academics. After three months of observation, the principal called her father in and suggested that he should take his children to another school where the bilingual program might serve them better. Her father refused the principal's idea and persisted in keeping his children there on the grounds that they would learn English faster without speaking their native language.

At home, her father called her and her sister and brothers in for a brief talk. He asked his children to put more effort in learning and listening and especially in communicating with other good students. He also asked the nuns of Saint Joseph Convent to provide language classes for his children after school. After five months, and with help from the nuns of Saint Joseph Convent, Anna gradually could understand what was going on in class and catch up to her classmates' level. In fifth grade, she could read better and better. With encouragement from the nuns, the teachers, and her parents, she spent more and more time reading and soon fell in love with books.

Once the bridge of communication was built, she made friends with most of the girls in her class and maintained those friendships for years after.

2

By seventh grade, Anna had acquired much familiarity with the American way of life, was making good progress as a student, and had made many friends. One of her closest friends, Cathy T., invited Anna and another girl to spend the night one weekend. There were three young ladies: Anna and two friends. They went down in the basement to play all kinds of games. Bored, they turned to a Ouija board. Anna had never heard of such a game, let alone played it. She then was instructed by the other two girls how to play. She became excited when her friends told her that the board could read and tell about her future. Anna agreed to participate, doing whatever her friends told her to do. At first, she did not believe the piece of heart-shaped wood moved itself, thinking that her friends were moving it . . . until she put her fingers on it.

She felt something like a light force pulling her finger along the board. Her friends asked the board many questions and seemed happy with the answers. They urged Anna to ask the board questions, any kind of questions, telling her that the board would answer immediately.

In order to test for any deception or cheating of the game, Anna tentatively asked, "What date, month, and year I was born?"

"You were born on October 30, 1966."

Anna was very sure before asking that none of her friends knew her birth date, but the board told it exactly right. Roused by curiosity, she asked, "In the future, what I will be?"

"A medical doctor," the answer came.

The board told her that the words were coming from the soul of a man named John. She was stunned, because she had wanted to be a doctor from her very young age. When hearing the enthusiasm of her friends, Anna just humbly said, "I don't believe it."

As a newcomer to the United States of America with little knowledge of the new country and not much experience in English, Anna may have thought that her friends wondered how she could dream of becoming a doctor. Though being interested in science, in fact she herself was not sure whether she could become a doctor or not.

She came home after the sleepover, trying very hard to forget the experience with the Ouija board, but the game kept coming back to bother her again and again. What was it in the game? What directed the board in answering her questions and those of her friends? Was that the real soul or spirit of someone named John, or was it the devil pretending to be John?

She dared not tell her grandparents or parents about it, because it was a great sin to believe in something other that what was taught by her belief system. Her grandmother had assured her that there were no wandering souls in the other world. Though she still thought of herself as a devout Catholic, other thoughts about life after death began to creep into her mind.

One afternoon, Anna decided to talk to her uncle, one of her father's brothers whom she felt she could talk to. To her surprise, her uncle admitted that he and even her mother had played with a Ouija board several times when they were young. When she asked if he believed in either wandering souls or devils speaking from the board, her uncle told her his story.

"Three other young students and I came together at a friend's house in the evening when the parents were absent. We played with the Ouija board after we were tired of other activities. Right at the beginning of the play, one soul took over, telling us her name and date of death and showing us how to reach her tomb inside the cemetery not far from my friend's house. After the game, in order to test the truth of what she had told us, the next day my friends and I all followed her directions, and we reached a tomb that matched the information the board gave us.

"I could not understand all of this and could not tell you if it was her or something else. Later we quit playing it, because the last time we played at the same place, something entered and called itself a devil. We tried very hard to expel it, but it persisted to resist our effort. We were scared and ran away. Later some older person told us the Ouija board was evil and we should stay away. We never played it since.

"Your mother also had several times participated in a group that played it and quit after the soul of her own grandpa came down and told her that this kind of game was evil and that she would lose her soul to Satan if she continued doing so."

Her uncle's story made Anna somewhat confused, but she was not convinced to believe in the game completely. However, she was in an equivocal mood. At one time, she ascribed it as evil, but at another, she tried to find a way to explain the game scientifically as the effect of an electromagnetic force combined with those who drove the board with the answers in their minds.

The simple event of spending a night at her friend's house had driven her to thinking more and more about an important matter: the spiritual life, or life after death. At her young age, she pondered other questions: Where had she come from? What exactly was the purpose of her life? Where were heaven and hell? These unanswered questions haunted her head almost every day, but she just kept them to herself, not daring to ask anyone.

3

Facing many difficulties—language, culture, skills, and education—Anna's parents had at first worked all kinds of odd jobs to support their four children. Then another child came: Jerome Vu, born in January 1976. He was named after Sister Mary Jerome of Saint Joseph Convent. Three days after coming to Wichita, her parents had their first job interview at Saint Joseph Hospital. Immediately, her mother was hired to work in the laundry department, where her job was to clean, fold, and iron the linens for surgery.

At his interview, her father was asked, "What had you been doing in Vietnam?"

"As a naval officer," he answered, "two things I can do, which are shooting the guns and navigation of a ship."

"Wichita lies in the middle of the United States," the interviewer replied. "There is no need for a gun shooter, neither for a navigator. However, you are hired, and I welcome you aboard. You should report to the hospital tomorrow morning at six o'clock sharp to begin your first day of work, and good luck to you."

The next morning, waking up at four thirty, Anna's father dressed and put on a tie. He walked into the hospital, expecting an interesting and good job. He was met by a lady and taken to the housekeeping department. His very first job in the United States was to mop the floors, sweep the halls, vacuum the room carpets, and clean the toilets.

Her parents were paid $2.65 per hour; the minimum wage was $2.45 at the time. With five children to take care of, her parents had no other choice than to accept the humble salaries and jobs that were offered. Three months later, Anna's father obtained work as a teacher's aid for a school and began taking night classes at a local college. He earned a bachelor's degree in mathematics and a master's in counseling. By choosing to teach mathematics and learning counseling, he aimed more at helping his children than building a career at the age of forty.

With the counseling background, he often discussed and

planned with his children for what they could become after they graduated from high school. By probing into each child's knowledge and vocational orientation, he advised each one of his children which career he or she should take to succeed in the United States of America.

Anna's parents valued education very highly and placed high expectations on their children, but their earnings were so humble that they were unable to make ends meet, let alone live up to their expectations. However, they determined to do whatever they could for their children. They discussed with them what they must do and the courses they should follow.

For the first few years in the United States, they demanded that the children put most of their efforts into learning English in order to keep up with schoolwork. There was no television watching during the weekdays—only on Friday and Saturday evenings. Lights out was at ten thirty every evening. When the children reached age fourteen, they were expected to get a part-time job after school or on weekends to help their parents. Anna began to work for Dairy Queen at thirteen years old by changing her birth year on her birth certificate; she worked at many other places, always trying to assist her parents in providing for the family.

From grade nine onward, Anna's father required agreement between himself and each child before enrolling in or changing classes. Prior to registration, he discussed with his children their goals for their careers and helped them choose their classes accordingly. Before going to college, each child in the family knew exactly what he or she had determined to become. The oldest, Anna's sister, declared without hesitation that she would be a dentist. She then enrolled in predental classes and was admitted into dentistry school after finishing her sophomore year in college. She received her DDS degree at twenty-four years of age.

When her turn came, Anna told her father, "I do not know if I am intelligent enough for what I want to be."

"What is it, a professor or a doctor?" her father teased.

"Since a very young age, I have loved to pretend to be a doctor, examining my playmates as they pretended to be my patients. At school in Vietnam, all my teachers knew my intention and encouraged me to pursue it. I think the seed of my career was sown in me since my childhood. However, the situation is changed now. We came to this country not very long ago and do not speak the new language well, much less writing and reading it. I am afraid that I may not graduate from college, let alone make it into medical school."

Thinking awhile, her father then said, "If that is the only thing you'd like to be, be firm on it. You may take longer to achieve your goal, but sooner or later, you will make it."

"I have not been thinking about anything else. Besides, there is something like a mysterious force urging me to the medical field, especially after playing the Ouija game. It was strange; I have had many repeating dreams in which I play the role of medicine lady in a faraway land, prescribing herbs to cure the sick."

Looking to see if her grandmother was around, Anna continued, "I talked to Grandmother about my wish and my dreams, and she disagreed. For a girl like me to go into the medical field, it takes a very long time for study. Once becoming a doctor, that girl would be very old for her marriage. However, Grandma took my dreams very seriously. She said that there must be some kind of link between me and the medicine man of the Vu clan of long ago, that this must have something to do with my wish and dreams. She told me that if I want to know, I should ask you, Dad, or read the Vu family history book.

"There is another coincidence: our family was sponsored by a hospital. From the first time walking into the hospital to learn English, I had a feeling that this place would be where I will work, and I heard a soundless voice calling and telling me that many sick people are waiting for me.

"Dad, I was born in the war, and I have been close to death many times. I have seen the dead, the wounded, the sick, and the hungry, all of their troubles inflicted by the war. The voice I heard may come from these poor miserable beings or probably from Divinity.

"I know I am not a smart person, but I have confidence that with God's help, I will make it into medical school."

When Anna stopped talking, her father went to his bedroom and came back quickly with a family registry book. He handed it to Anna and said, "I do not believe in the connection between ancestors and you, but you and people of your generation have the opportunity to mend the broken medical line of the Vu clan. I want you to read the story of a man whose survival made possible the continuation of our existence now. He was very talented in Oriental medicine. If you determine to become a physician, you should consider gaining more knowledge of Asian ways of treatments, such as using herbs and acupuncture. Besides, I and your ancestors will be very happy when the line of medicine in our clan will flow again."

Anna read the book and was happier because of her ancestral roots than for the continuation of the medicine line. She read:

Most members of the Vu clan were medicine men and Christians who lived peacefully in a village of North Vietnam. In 1790 a new, young king of Vietnam was enthroned, and he had a deep hatred for Christians. Upon coming to the crown, he decreed that all Christians must be destroyed. Once again, the Christians were killed or went into hiding.

It was during this time that the Vu clan faced persecution. Some Vu family members left the village; some were captured and imprisoned. One of the prisoners was Con Vu, a single man of twenty-five years of age. As fate would have it, he was still waiting for his trial after six months of imprisonment. Being strong and young, he was brought to work in the warden's garden.

While working in front of the house, he observed some sort of commotion inside and outside the house: people came and went away. Their faces seemed grave and worried. Con Vu also smelled a strong odor of medicine in the air. He sensed that someone must be very sick in this household. On the one hand, as a man of medicine, he was curious to know what was going on, but on the other hand, as a prisoner, he had no right to ask questions, especially about the warden's business. As the days went on, his medical skill and curiosity pushing him, he finally approached one of the friendlier guards to see what the matter was with the warden's family. From this guard, he learned that the only son of the warden was very sick. The warden had invited many famous doctors to come examine his son. They prescribed all kinds of medicine and herbs for him, but none helped. Instead, the situation got worse day after day, and the warden was in despair.

"Could you ask the warden," Con Vu said, "to give me permission to just look at his son? I am a medicine man myself. Hopefully I might be able to help him."

"No," said the guard, "you have no right whatsoever to ask anything."

"It does not do any harm if I just examine the boy. I just want to help and ask no favor in return."

The guard then became quiet and reflective.

That night Con Vu was called in to see the warden at his office.

"I have learned that you have helped many people in your area with your herbs, and you have asked to see my son."

"Yes, sir."

"Tell me what and how you know about medicine."

Con Vu then related to the warden how he met his teacher and had been with him for more than five years. During this period, he had gained knowledge of the symptoms, causes, and treatments of most common and even rare illnesses. "When I was eleven years old, my mother suddenly fell ill. Her illness became worse and worse until one day she could not talk or eat. She was throwing up right after swallowing her food. After about three weeks, she was very slim and pale, but the scariest thing was that her body became partially numbed. Many doctors examined her, but no one could find out her cause of illness. At eleven years old, I had no idea how gravely ill my mother was. Then one day I happened to overhear my father's conversation with my uncle about preparation for my mother's funeral. Of course I loved my mother very much and I never thought that she would die and be away from me. Quietly, I went to her room, sat beside her, and looked at her lying unconscious on her bed. I called to her, but she did not respond. Then I touched her hands and found that they were cold and had no feeling at all. I knew now that she was going to die. I cried in silence and walked out of the room. With sadness, I got out of the house and wandered to the village gate. I came and sat behind a banyan tree and cried by myself. I did not know for how long I had been sitting there. I did not want to go home, for I was afraid of seeing my mother dying.

"'Why are you crying?' asked a voice.

"I turned and saw an old man about sixty-five years of age. I told him about my mother dying. He looked at me, saying, 'You are a good son, but tell me how you know that your mother is dying.'

"'My father said so, and I know it, too, sir.'

"'Where is your house?' asked the old man.

"I pointed in the direction of my house and told him, 'Right over there, sir.'

"'I happened to pass by this way and heard your crying,' said the man. 'I thought you were an abandoned child. No, you're not a child, but a young man crying for his mother who is dying. You act and talk like a fine boy from a well-raised family. Could you take me to your house and let me look at your mother? I am a medicine man.'

"I stared at him without knowing what to do. He smiled at me, touched my head, and then grabbed my arms to pull me up. We both walked home. When we arrived there, my father and my uncle were gone, probably to arrange for my mother's funeral. I led the old man to my mother's bed. He grabbed her hands and felt her pulse for a rather long moment. Then he opened wide the windows to get light so he could see my mother's face, mouth, and tongue. He asked for a cup of water.

"From his bosom, he pulled a package full of medicines and mixed some of them into water. He then raised my mother's head up and forced the mixture into her mouth and down her throat. About fifteen minutes later, I touched my mother's hands and felt warmth, not cold as before. Her breast began moving up and down, lightly and regularly.

"The old medicine man walked out of the room and asked me to bring him ink, brush, and paper. He wrote on paper what I thought would be a prescription.

"'Give this to your father,' he told me. 'When he reads this, he will know who I am. Tell him to buy all these herbs, soak them in three big bowls of water, then condense them into one small bowl. Help her to drink it in three days. Your mother will not die. She is lucky that I met you. It is God's will that it happens. I will be back in three days on my way back from my planned destination.'

"When my father read the prescription with the old man's name on it, his face beamed with joy.

"'Oh my God! I have been looking for him all over and I could not find him. Fortunate that he came by.'

"My father was so happy when I told him how I had met the old man.

"Three days later, he appeared at my house. During these three days, my mother was recovering rapidly. She could sit up in bed and talk a little. Three weeks later, she could resume routine, light work around the house.

"The coming of the old man turned my life around. His name was Han V. Lee, a genius in Oriental medicine. His house was deep in the mountains of Ninh Binh province. He was like a cloud floating all over the country. He wanted me to become his medical student. My parents were happy to send me with him. I stayed, learned, and traveled with him for more than five years. He transferred most of his medicinal knowledge to me with the command that I learn it to help the sick, not to become rich from it. Like him, I carry with me all the time some herbs so that they can be used at any time to save people.

"My teacher sent me home when he saw the fit moment. He told me not to come back to look for him unless he sent for me. I have never heard from him since. I practiced medicine in my area until I was brought here."

There was a light of hope in the warden's eyes after listening to Con Vu's story. With a weary tone, he described his son's illness. "My only son is named Than Nguyen. He is twelve years old and has always been an intelligent, strong, happy, and handsome boy. Last month, I brought my family to my grandfather's anniversary at my uncle's home in Bac Ninh province. We stayed there for two days, during which my son played on the swings and ate all kinds of food and fruits. He was very happy to be there and everyone loved him. I was so proud of him and had great hope in my son's future. Just one day after we returned home, suddenly his body began to shake, followed by a high fever. Every six hours, the shaking and fever repeated again and again. His body now is just a skeleton, because he can't eat anything but a couple of spoons of porridge that we force into his stomach every day. His breath is so weak now that it cannot even flutter a candle flame. I have brought in so many doctors who have given my son so many kinds of medicines and herbs, but my son's sickness remains uncured and even the cause of it is unknown. My son is my hope, my happiness. He is everything to me and my family. I would trade everything I have to save him. Now, I am desperate. That is why I seek your help, and you are my last hope."

The warden stopped. The room was quiet; only a few breaths were heard. After a long moment, he continued, "I call you tonight not as a warden to a detainee, but as a poor father with a dying son whom he loves dearly. And you, not as a prisoner, but as a medical doctor that I have heard good things from. Please do not humble yourself, but tell me: Can you save my son, or not?"

"I do not know, sir," said Con Vu. "I may know something after examining your son, if I am allowed to."

With hope in his eyes, the warden secretly brought Con Vu to his son's bedside during the night. After examining the boy, his tongue, his excrement and urine, and feeling his pulse, Con Vu prescribed a list of medicines and said, "If the following things happen after he takes the medicines, then we have hope: his temperature shoots up high at first, the body shakes strongly for about three minutes, then stops. The cycles of shaking will repeat about every thirty minutes along with lower temperature, and the shaking will become weaker each time. In about three hours, the shaking will come to a stop and the body temperature will become normal.

Between the shaking episodes, the boy might vomit, have a bowel movement, or urinate."

It happened as Con Vu had anticipated. Being reassured, the warden was calm watching his son shaking, vomiting, and urinating. Then everything came to a complete stop. His son slept peacefully. His breast moved up and down regularly. After five prescriptions, the son of the warden could sit up, smile, and talk to his father. The warden's house was filled with joy again.

However, as his son recovered, the warden became more and more troubled. He did not know how to compensate Con Vu. He did not want Con Vu to be dropped into the ocean at night, as the other Christians had been, but he did not know how to rescue him, either. In his humble position, he could not set him free. He called Con Vu one night and told him that he wanted to help him escape, but he could not think of the best way to do it.

After thinking a while, Con Vu asked the warden, "Do you have the power to bury a body of a prisoner who dies of a dangerous disease?"

"Yes." The next day it was reported that Con Vu had contracted cholera and died. To avoid the spread of the contagious disease, the warden ordered that the body had to be buried immediately at one designated place. Con Vu's corpse was carried away and buried in a shallow hole at night. When the soldiers who buried him had left the grave, two men came from the warden's house and dug him up. They brought him to a place where, about four o'clock in the morning, he woke up and quietly left.

Discreetly, he wandered around his old village and found no relatives there. The executions of Christians were taking place all over Vietnam, severe at some times and less so at others. Many European missionaries were imprisoned and executed throughout this time. In 1858, the French used this as one of the main reasons to invade Vietnam: on the pretext of stopping the persecutions. The sounds of the French guns in 1858 actually foretold the Vietnam War, more than a hundred years later.

Con Vu kept moving around and at last he ended up hiding in the place that is now called Nam Dinh. He earned his living by bartering his medicines for food. People loved him and protected him. No one questioned who he was. He married and had two sons and three daughters. One of his sons became a medicine man. Medical careers were passed down to successive generations, but were cut off by a man named Khoan Vu in the early days of the twentieth century. This man dictated, "Anyone who lacks the qualifications required for this career would be a murderer instead of a medicine man." He burned most of his medicine books when he perceived that none of his four sons met his qualifications to become men of medicine."

4

Reading the story of her ancestor gave Anna a clear picture of Vietnamese life more than two hundred years before and shed light on her roots as well. These persecutions and sufferings led to French domination over Vietnam and then to many wars, including the Vietnam War.

After graduation from Garden City High School, where her father worked as mathematics teacher, Anna was sent to Saint Mary of the Plains, a small Catholic college in Dodge City, Kansas, only fifty miles east of Garden City. The school was founded by Saint Joseph Convent, of which Mother Mary Ann McNamara, who had sponsored the family's coming to Wichita, Kansas, in 1975, was the mother superior. As a private college, its tuition and boarding cost more than public schools. Anna's parents could not afford to pay for all the costs, so Anna had to work to pay for about half of all expenses. Scholarships and grants paid for the rest.

Anna stayed very devout in her beliefs. She knelt and prayed every night before going to bed. Mostly she prayed for her big family to be in good health and at peace. And she also prayed on her own behalf. Her enrollment in premed courses conjured up in her memory the Ouija board game in her friend's basement more than five years earlier, almost completely forgotten by this time. She wondered if the Ouija board really knew her future and read her mind. Or was it just a coincidence? Then, not even certain she would make it into medical school, she brushed it aside. Anna thought of herself as having average intelligence, but she wanted to believe in things that were explainable.

One night in bed after praying, she suddenly realized there were many things she could not prove; she could only believe in them for the sake of her soul. She strongly believed she possessed a soul, but she wondered where God took it from and when God planted it into the body. She pondered, "Where do you lie, my soul? In my mind, my heart, my brain, or my whole body? Do you carry with you the original sin before you enter the physical body? Are you an accomplice for all the sins committed by my body? Who is in control? Is it you or my body that is to blame for my daily transgressions?"

5

In spite of working to pay for almost half of her expenses at school, Anna maintained a grade-point average close to 4.0, all the while remaining faithful to her beliefs and routine prayers. She loved music and found time to play violin. She chose as electives music classes taught by Dr. Phillip Dexter; studying music enabled her to enjoy life and eased the stresses of college life. Once in a while, with classmates, she stayed after class to consult with Dr. Dexter about music composition. Sometimes their discussions strayed to other issues such as life after death. Dr. Dexter often mentioned that he had learned music from previous lives and that he really believed in reincarnation of human beings.

Anna did not believe in reincarnation, and she told Dr. Dexter so, and she told him that she believed in God and in life after death because human beings have a soul.

One evening during her last year at Saint Mary of the Plains, at about ten thirty, sitting at her desk and studying for a chemistry test, Anna suddenly felt a chill all over her body, and her eyes became blurred with some vague, faraway fog. She seemed to see the image of Dr. Dexter floating in midair for about ten seconds, then disappearing in the fog. It was not quite like seeing, but some kind of vision took place in her mind. While shaking her head to rid herself of what she thought was a delusion, her phone rang; Dr. Dexter was on the line. He told Anna outright that he just had a meditation and that his soul phased out and met Anna's.

That was the first time in her life that Anna had heard the word "meditation" in English. She asked Dr. Dexter what meditation meant and what it was about. It took awhile for him to explain what it was all about and what he was doing. Anna was shocked as she listened to Dr. Dexter tell her that during his meditation, his soul could get out of his body to meet hers. Anna did not care about his or his soul's purpose for the meeting; she knew that what he said was contrary to her belief that only when one is dead does the soul escape the body. She wondered whether she should trust what her professor was telling her. Reflecting on the several times he had mentioned that he had learned music from his previous lives, Anna now understood what he had been saying.

Meeting with Dr. Dexter after their next class, Anna asked him more about his meditation and why he had made contact with her instead of another. Dr. Dexter simply stated that Anna had the same frequencies as his in a world other than this. He added that this kind of meeting could be called sixth-sense or telepathic communication, or whatever other name she chose. He told Anna to flash back to the early days of the twentieth century to recall how communications among people took place and the ways in which they were able to make contact with each other. He then suggested that one hundred years from the present, communication would be far more advanced. Meditation was the science that Eastern civilization had discovered thousands of years ago, he told her. It was both a means for maintaining health and a means to communicate among the souls of this world and with spiritual beings of other heavenly worlds.

Anna marveled at Dr. Dexter's sayings. She asked him if he had been making any spiritual contact with other beings and whether they had the same feelings as humans. Dr. Dexter responded that he had many contacts in the spiritual worlds, where there was no need to know to what world they belonged. He added that the science of this physical world assumes that human beings are endowed with the five senses we all know: seeing, hearing, touching, feeling, and tasting. They provide the general ideas as we try to make sense of what is going on in our life.

"In reality," he told her, "there are a lot more than five senses, and there are so many different kinds and levels in each sense. Take for instance the sense of taste. The same food may bring a different flavor to different persons—or to different animals. Among human beings, some have stronger senses than others. Some animals experience far more different smells and tastes than human beings. In vision, most animals fare far better than human beings. Many animals can see things that human beings consider invisible." He suggested that if someone saw something out of the ordinary, our tendency would be to attribute this to hallucination or drug influence. But it could be that the person was simply exercising a sense that others lacked.

Anna was not sure that she agreed completely with Dr. Dexter, but his ideas had nevertheless greatly changed the course of her thinking about this life—and the life after.

6

As she prepared for the Medical College Admission Test (MCAT), Anna had to brush aside these unanswered questions and study very hard, hoping to get a high score. Unfortunately, her test scores were not very high above the national average, and that made her road into medical school rougher. After her interview by the board of admission, she was at first admitted into medical school as the last name on the list, but later she received a denial letter. She would later learn that her place had been given to another minority student who was far less qualified than Anna, but more important. Anna's name was taken out of the list and not even placed on the waiting list, and no one cared enough to tell her why.

Anna was devastated and disappointed. However, she consoled herself that God might not have wanted her to be a doctor. She enrolled in a PhD program in biochemistry and molecular genetics and forgot about medical school. She made beautiful progress in the PhD program and planned to finish her PhD degree in four years. And suddenly she got a call to come to the University of Kansas School of Medicine. The unknown force inside her again pushed her back into medical school, and she accepted it.

The years of medical school did not go smoothly for Anna. At the end of the first year, her grandmother was very sick. She had lung cancer and was diagnosed as terminal. She had difficulty breathing and had to be hospitalized. She wanted Anna to be with her, especially at the last moment of her life. Though busy at the time, Anna came to visit her grandmother every week. When the doctor informed them of her imminent death, the whole family gathered with Anna's grandmother in the hospital to wait for the time, but she stayed stable until very late. Hoping that she was not going to pass away during the night, everyone else went home and left Anna with her dying grandmother.

Anna's parents went to her uncle's house and rested in a basement bedroom. Fatigued and sad, Anna's mother fell asleep quickly after lying down. Anna's father, still awake, tried to shake his wife awake when he heard her loud babbling, apparently in a dream.

Once awake, she told her husband in an urgent voice, "Your mother just passed by here and stood at the head of the bed, wearing a dazzling white dress. It seemed she wanted to say good-bye or say something to me. I may have found out what she wanted to tell me if you had not waked me up."

"It was just a dream. Go back to sleep," Anna's father responded.

"I know it was in my dream, but it was so real to me."

Just then the telephone rang. It was Anna calling from the hospital to inform them of her grandmother's death.

At the last second of her life, Anna's grandmother had opened her eyes, squeezed Anna's hands, smiled, and passed away. It was at this very moment, as they later learned, that Anna's mother claimed to see her pass to say good-bye at Anna's uncle's house in Wichita, Kansas.

Another strange thing was her dream: Anna's mother saw her grandmother wearing the clothes chosen for her by the uncle before he went home.

That was the second time Anna's mother had such a dream. The first one had taken place nine years earlier. She had dreamed that her mother in Vietnam had died and had come to the United States to tell her daughter, Anna's mother, that she had passed away. Anna's mother had cried and run after her mother, jumping over her husband. Upon waking, she tearfully told her husband about the dream. Because of the difficulty of correspondence between the United States and Vietnam at that time, it took several weeks to receive the bad news confirming her mother's death, which was concurrent with the dream Anna's mother had had.

Her grandmother's death depressed Anna very much, because the two of them had shared a strong bond since Anna's childhood. She loved her grandmother and admired her very much, and she believed that no woman had been greater or endured a more difficult life than her grandmother.

One day, at the sickbed in the hospital, Anna's grandmother

had related what was going on during her life in the course of the Vietnam War.

> *I was born and raised in the countryside in a family with high dignity and merit five years before World War I. As a girl, I was not allowed access to school; I had to stay at home to learn what would be necessary to be a consummate wife. One day when I was seventeen years old, my father informed me of my coming marriage. Regardless of my protest as being too young and having no clue about whom I was going to marry, he went on to tell me that everything had been arranged and taken care of. There were no more questions about it. I stood stupefied for a while, then walked to my room and lay down with tears in my eyes. I did not want to get married, but I could not refuse to obey my father. I had no choice.*
>
> *Two weeks later, I became the wife of the man who is your grandfather now.*
>
> *When I came to his house, my mother-in-law had been sick in bed for weeks. Many medicine men had come and gone. None of them could cure her. Later I learned that she had a kind of ovarian cancer. Anticipating that she would die soon, my husband's father demanded that his son take a wife at once to take care of his younger children and family business. Otherwise it would have to wait, because tradition would not allow any marriage in the family within three years of the death of one of the parents.*
>
> *On the day of wedding, my mother-in-law could not even sit straight up on her sickbed to look at her daughter-in-law. She just groped for the bride's hands, a difficult smile on her withering lips.*

She died five days after her son's wedding. I became the surrogate mother of my husband's sisters and brother.

Willingly or not, I became the major lady of a big family from the first day of my marriage. There was not even a second of romance or honeymoon. The only happiness for me was to get everything in order: keeping track of the workers in the rice field, house chores, food for everyone, and so on. Usually, I was the one who would be the last going to bed at night and the first to wake up in the early morning.

Probably because I was burdened by the hard and heavy load of work, I had several miscarriages before your father was born and survived, and then two of your uncles followed several years later.

The hardest time was right after the onset of World War II. Under oppression of both the French and the Japanese and high taxes, the Vietnamese were living under many restrictions, and starvation killed millions of people. My family and I went through several weeks without food, but thank God, we survived.

Right after the famine came the revolution of communism. My husband did not help me much with the family business during this episode. He was involved with some sort of politics and was away most of the time. Then he was in hiding and in prison off and on, and I had to manage everything, including feeding him while he was in jail. Besides the daily drudgery, I also experienced worries and harassment from the local officials for being the wife of a conspirator, especially when he was released and then escaped into the French quarter. The war between the communists and the French dragged on until the Geneva agreement to divide Vietnam into two parts: the North for those who chose socialism, and the

South for democracy. With determination, my husband took your father to the South, regardless of what would be happening to me and his two sons still living in his native village in the North.

The news of their departure came to me much later, when there were only two weeks left until the last chance for anyone in the North to go to the South, as established in Geneva. The communist guards were blocking access, but I knew it was urgent to decide whether to stay or go with my husband. Staying would mean breaking up my family for good, but going meant my life would be shattered by leaving my native place.

On the way home from the rice field I slowly walked to the gate of the village. The sun was setting. The beautiful surroundings held me back. I stopped and stood under the shade of a banyan tree and was mesmerized by the sound of the flute coming from a big kite silhouetted against the blue evening sky. The field was full of golden ears of rice fluttering and murmuring in the breeze. The sounds were the best kind of music, bringing happiness and prosperity to the villagers. My visions were of everything about this place: the ponds full of fish; the green, thick hedges of bamboo that ran endlessly around the village. The river and the hedges were like moats and great walls to protect my village from predators. But most important were the flat, far-stretched rice fields that had been nourishing the villagers from generation to generation.

The dark gradually closed around me and I saw a shadow coming. It was the husband of my niece, who wanted to inform me of something. When close enough, I heard him say, "You are in danger, because your son is a spy for the Americans." He hurriedly walked away to avoid notice by others.

With help from this man, I quietly gave away or sold anything I could and sneaked out of the village in the night. Being warned of the roadblock, I brought your two uncles to the coastal village, where I paid some ounces of gold to a man to take us by raft to the coast. Fortunately, we were picked up by an American ship and brought to the South to reunite with my husband and my son, your father."

She stopped speaking, but Anna knew the rest.

In the South, Anna's grandmother had worked all kinds of odd jobs, often working fourteen hours a day in order to raise her children and send them to school. Once in the United States, her wish would have been to visit her beautiful native village in North Vietnam just once again, and Anna had promised her grandmother that she would buy her the airplane tickets and accompany her on that trip after graduating from medical school. Never did that plan materialize, because Anna's grandmother fell ill while Anna was struggling with the hardest years of medical school.

But Anna's biggest regret later was that she should have listened to her grandmother's advice not to marry the man Anna brought home to meet the whole family. Far in the future, when she found out that her grandmother had been right, it was too late to say anything at all to her. Anna would meet this man in medical school and would marry him against her grandmother's will right after graduation and before plunging into her career as a physician. They would have two children, one boy and one girl.

After her grandmother's funeral, Anna fell ill, but the worst part was that she lost her enthusiasm for schooling. She was experiencing weight loss and even memory loss as well. The medical school allowed her a one-year leave of absence for treatment. At this difficult time, Anna considered quitting medical school. But her grandmother came to her dreams again and again, and each time she told Anna that everything would be fine and that she must go back to medical school to fulfill her task in this world.

CHAPTER 3
JOURNEYS OF REMORSE, JOURNEYS OF HEALING

I

Anna succeeded in becoming a doctor. The war and fate had brought her from the small city of a faraway country through many terrifying experiences to the United States, where she faced hardship and difficulties while becoming a physician. It had been a long journey. But looking ahead, she realized that the real long journey was about to begin: a journey of her body and her soul.

Throughout her years of medical school, Anna had witnessed so much suffering from disease. She had been caretaker for many dying patients. Though they died from different causes, all dying persons shared one common fear: the fear of death. They tried to cling to this world and asked Anna to save their lives, because they did not know what would be waiting for them once they passed. In most circumstances, Anna had to take on the role of a chaplain or a psychiatrist to calm dying patients and make them believe that death was not the end and that there would be a beautiful life after it.

At the moment, Anna strongly believed in God, the soul, and life after death and perceived that she was destined to become a physician. She believed that her task was not just to save a patient's life but also to prepare them, when the time came, to go to the next world without any fear. The best way to reduce fear of death, she told them, was to believe in the benevolence of God, who would take the dying believer in his hands. Anna wished to learn more about how to prepare them to go peacefully into eternity beyond this world.

Even so, Anna still had no firm ideas about life after death. But she did remember many of her mother's dreams and other strange, unexplained things taking place on the maternal side of her family. She wondered about the true path of the soul when it leaves the physical body. Her interest in life after death ebbed and flowed for some time, but it was strongly in her mind at the moment, as were her conversations with Dr. Dexter.

Anna was also concerned about communication between the living and the dead. Once beyond, is there any channel of communication between the two worlds? She wondered whether in some way the souls of her living mother and dead grandmother had met, as it seemed from her mother's dream. Anna was determined to observe, investigate, and keep records of anything related to the mysterious paths of life after death, hoping that something would shed a light on a scientific explanation for communication with the souls and heavenly roads taken after leaving this suffering world. Beginning with her years of internship and continuing through her profession as a physician, Anna encountered peculiarities and phenomena in the journey of body and soul that went beyond her ability to explain.

2

After graduating from the University of Kansas School of Medicine and equipped with the zeal, confidence, and enthusiasm of a young, newly graduated physician, Anna was interviewed by eighteen medical institutions. She was fatefully matched to the University of Kansas Internal Medicine Residency Program, working part-time at the Kansas City Veterans Affairs Medical Center in Missouri, where she would work with many patients who had been involved in the Vietnam War.

She was very glad at first, thinking that it was a predestined mission for her as a Vietnamese to meet and help to heal many Vietnam vets. She hoped she could learn more about the American soldiers during the time of fighting and after the war. She had read that unlike other US vets who were welcomed home and appreciated and respected, the Vietnam vets had faced rejection and hostility. Anna hoped to bring some consolation to these honorable patients.

After just a few days, however, she thought that working at a veterans hospital must be harder than at other places. Besides the hardship of being an intern and not sleeping enough, she faced much pressure from the patients. Many of them blamed their illnesses on Vietnam and harbored a hatred for Vietnamese, noncommunists as well as communists. From the beginning, there was mistrust between Anna and her patients. Some patients said to her face that they did not want a Vietnamese to touch their body, even if she was a doctor. At first, she was angry and frustrated, but she needed to deal with this problem in order to succeed. Immediately and strongly, she was determined to find a way to deal with them.

In a voice of authority, she told them, "I am all you have, Vietnamese or not. It's up to you whether or not you want to be helped. If you would rather decline my help and die, then so be it." Anna paused some seconds to check their reaction. She then continued, "I do have rules if you wish to be treated. I treat you with respect; I expect respect in return. If this is violated, you will be escorted out of the hospital. I will not tolerate aggression while you are in my care." Surprised by her harsh and strong will, some became docile and submissive to whatever she ordered them to do.

Among the Vietnam vets, some hated Vietnamese for cheating them while in Vietnam: some had their property stolen, some contracted sexually transmitted diseases from Vietnamese hookers, and some vets had picked up the stereotype that the Vietnamese were sneaky. Anna did the best she could to explain to these vets that they had not met the real Vietnamese. Those they had met and thought of as typical Vietnamese were really victims of the long war; they stuck close to the US soldiers during the war to get the most out of them. If they wanted to meet the real Vietnamese, Anna told them, they needed to contact more Vietnamese in the United States or to go to Vietnam again and look for someone who was not trying to get something from them. One of the vets did travel back to Vietnam with a church mission, stayed in Vietnam, and married a young Vietnamese woman there.

Late one Sunday afternoon when Anna was about to go home after more than thirty-six hours on duty without a single minute of sleeping, an ambulance rushed in, transporting a Vietnam vet who was having kidney failure. Anna forgot about going home and rushed in to rescue the unconscious patient. He gradually regained consciousness and was hospitalized under her care. At first, he just stared at her with contempt and did not answer her questions.

He demanded, "Let me talk to the doctor."

"I am your doctor," she replied.

He remained silent for a long moment, then asked, "Are you Vietnamese?"

"Yes, I am," she answered.

Anna waited for his response, but he stayed silent.

"Is there anything the matter with being Vietnamese?" Anna pushed for an answer.

"I hate the Vietnamese," he retorted curtly.

Anna pretended not to hear what he said and kept herself busy doing what she needed to do for him, a smile still on her face.

For two days, though pretending no notice of what Anna was doing for him, he sometimes stole a look and seemed angered by her smiling face.

One Wednesday morning after examining him, Anna found that his situation was improving. He could be released soon, and she needed to tell him something for fear that she would not have the chance to talk to him again. Before going out of the room, and with determination, she told him, "You may hate me as you will. I do not know the reasons why you hate Vietnamese, but I have nothing to do with what you think in your mind. Your heart seems full of spitefulness for Vietnam. It could be that you call yourself a victim of the Vietnam War and you blame Vietnamese for whatever harmed you, one way or the other.

"My brothers and sister and I were born and grew up in the war. My dad fought during the whole war. But we did not let the war ruin us while it ruined Vietnam. Surviving the war has brought us strength and perseverance. It was not the war that ruined you, but it is you who destroy yourself. Vietnamese people had nothing to do with your life, and now it is you who control it.

"Just think about how much the Vietnamese people suffered during the war and even after the war. How many millions turned into enemies of the new regime? How many other millions fled the country? Did they turn to drugs or alcohol to forget the hardships they had to endure? The answer is no. When the US government abandoned them, the South Vietnamese knew that they began with another war, the war of survival. They escaped the country, not for economic reasons only, but they risked their life on the dangerous ocean to defend the freedom the communists took away. They would rather die than live without freedom.

"Do you think that they are cowards? As a doctor who happens to be Vietnamese, I will take care of you and do my best to help you. Also, because of love of God, I do not mind a bit about your attitude and what you said. I will treat you with kindness and the conscience of a doctor toward a patient. If you are a Christian as I believe you are, you should pray that God will protect you and help you through the bad experiences that you have been enduring."

His name was Johnny W. Smith, and he was forty-six. During the time Johnny was in the hospital, as Anna stopped by his bed each day, she showed sympathy and concern for him. After a couple of days under her care, his attitude to her slowly seemed to change as his health improved. She discovered that in addition to his alcoholism, he was addicted to other drugs. Before dismissing him from the hospital, she told him that he should consider quitting alcohol and drugs if he wanted to survive. She warned him that no one could save his life if he came back here a second time. Before leaving the hospital, she called him into her office and told him especially that he should consider asking for the spiritual help from God in his prayers. He said nothing and left.

Just thirty-six days later he was brought into hospital again. By some coincidence of fate, Anna was again on duty. When they saw each other, both knew that there was no chance for him to go home anymore. Though very sick and weak, he could talk. He confessed that he had no bold determination to quit any of his bad habits. The only thing that changed him was coming back to God. He had prayed and asked God to forgive his sins and for his blaming problems on others.

One Sunday evening, in a trembling tone of voice, he confided his story to her.

> *I am a farmer and was born and raised on the farm. In 1965, I graduated from high school in the top 10 percent of my class of thirty-six students. In June of 1966, I was drafted and brought to Vietnam. I believed in the good cause: that I came to Vietnam to help South Vietnamese people to defend their freedom from the North's communists.*
>
> *Before leaving for Vietnam, I had dreamed of being a hero in the war. When I walked out of the airplane in Saigon, the sultry and humid weather made me sweat all over. I had two days in Saigon to wait for transportation to my assigned unit, stationed*

next to the Cambodian border. In the evening of the same day of my arrival, I had permission to go around Saigon. When I walked out of the camp gate, immediately a group of young Vietnamese rushed to me. They picked, nagged, pushed, and pulled me around and around. They asked me hundreds of questions:

"Do you need change money? Need a taxi? Where do you want to go? Do you need Coca-Cola? Do you need a girl?"

At this moment, I saw one US soldier walking toward me. The Vietnamese group stopped their movement and looked at the newcomer. It seemed they knew him well. He told the group to leave me alone and introduced himself to me as Jack Williams. He was stationed right inside the airport and had been in Vietnam almost ten months. He called a taxi and both of us hopped in; Jack had a plan. As we rode in the taxi, he told me everything bad and good about Saigon and Vietnam. He took me around some crowded streets of Saigon where Vietnamese and foreigners were walking around or sitting inside luxurious restaurants eating or drinking and laughing. It seemed to me that everyone was living in a peaceful time. There was no sign of war in the city.

Alongside some of the streets, the US products from the Army and Airforce Exchange Service were displayed for sale everywhere. I wondered how this stuff could be out of the PX. We stopped and ate some ice cream at the shop where we could see what Saigon was like in the afternoon.

The evening came and the streets became more crowded. Jack took me to a bar where he went frequently. There were many young, beautiful girls working as servers. They all wore traditional Vietnamese long dresses. When we came in, two young girls came out to welcome us. The one sitting with me had a beautiful name, Angela. She had a slender body and a lovely smile. Jack ordered beers. I had been drunk before after just two cans of beer. On this occasion, I drank one can after another as the girls brought them to the table.

As a student just out of high school, I wanted to prove that I was a man. I kept drinking until Jack knew that I could not drink anymore. Angela took me to a taxi, then to a hotel. I was not completely drunk, but the amount of beer was just enough to induce me to do many things that I would not do if I were sober. That was my first night out on the streets of Saigon. It was also the night I slept with a Vietnamese woman, who induced me to smoke marijuana so as to wake me and every part of my body up for the night with her that she hoped I would never forget.

At six o'clock the next morning, I dressed and Angela called a taxi for me. She took all the money I had, but I did not care at the moment. I went back to the camp with a body stricken with fatigue and a soul full of regret.

The next day, I was put in a convoy to my assigned unit station, about fifteen miles from the closest city. There were military operations most of the time.

All Vietnamese villagers lived in war zones. People got killed day and night by rockets, artillery, and gunfire from either side. Roads were mined, paths booby trapped, and houses burned. There was no way to know whether a Vietnamese was a friend or an enemy in such an area.

Our unit faced dangers daily, with rockets and missiles launched from the border areas. Our main task was to stop *infiltration of weapons and communist personnel from Cambodia. The enemy concentrated their efforts on destroying us or distracting us so that they could maintain the infiltration routes. After only two months, three men in my platoon were killed, and I wondered when my turn would be. I thought it was only a matter of days or weeks. I had no hope of going back home.*

I tried to forget about my death by using cocaine. Many soldiers did the same thing. Either they needed the courage to go on or to avoid thinking about the dangers waiting for them at any moment. Gradually, I went deeply into that substance, and I spent all my money on cocaine, which was easy to buy in that area.

Nine months after arriving in Vietnam, having the chance to come back to Saigon, I went to the bar where Angela worked. I was so happy to see her again, but she looked at me as though she had never met me before. I told her how we had met, but she persisted shaking her head, saying that she had never known me or met anyone like me. What hurt me the most was when she accused me of doing drugs, saying that a drug man had no money.

Her statement was true, but it made me hate Vietnamese women and Vietnamese people as well. I thought that I had come to Vietnam to defend them, but they had cheated me and treated me like dirt in return. By an irony of fate, I had survived many dangers when I did not care about my life anymore. I kept destroying my soul and body with more drugs and hookers.

Only twenty days before my term in Vietnam expired, I discovered I had contracted the most dangerous sexual disease, syphilis, and that made me even more careless about my life. I tried to forget it by drinking. Drinking and drugs were my friends, and Vietnam was my enemy. I hated everything about Vietnam; I blamed the Vietnamese for my troubles.

When I came back home, I spent the little money I made from farming on drugs and liquor. Wherever I went, people shunned me or looked at me like I was an animal. Most people in my area had the thought that all Vietnam vets had either one problem or the other.

I did not believe in anything, including God, since I was in Vietnam. God had abandoned people like me, I thought. Several of my friends were either dead or wounded. I was not wounded by the enemy's weapons, but by Vietnamese drugs, diseases, and alcohol. Now my liver and my kidneys are not functioning well. My body is just a gaunt skeleton, and my soul has been sinking in a sea of desperation and hatred. I hated Vietnamese, and I blamed them for all my problems. Without the Vietnam War or the Vietnamese, I might have a decent life like any other American man. When Vietnamese refugees came to the US, I hated them all. By living on a farm, I scarcely saw any Vietnamese. That helped my soul live in peace.

When awaking from the coma with you standing there, I thought I saw Angela again. It was she who first taught me the sweetness and the bitterness of life in Vietnam with which I began ruining my life. During the first week under your care, I treated you with contempt, hatred, and spitefulness in return for your care, sympathy, smiles, and forgiveness. Your attitude had a great effect on my thinking. Rechecking my opinions and my thoughts, for the first time I realized that my assumptions that all Vietnamese are bad was really wrong. For many days, after reflecting on my own life, I saw that I was dead wrong when I blamed all my problems on you, a Vietnamese.

You should despise us, but instead we despise you. You were traumatized by the war ever since you were born, and you all lived in a very difficult situation, but you did not allow the war to break you down. Then you came to this country with a lot of disadvantages, especially in language.

However, you have surpassed most of us to become a doctor. Your body is small, but your heart is big. Every day, I am just waiting to see you appearing at the room door with a smiling face, approaching me. Many times I have wanted to apologize and ask you for forgiveness, but I did not have the courage to do so. I have listened to you and decided to seek God and ask him for forgiveness as well. Please forgive me and pray for me.

Before his death, Johnny wanted to meet with newspaper reporters to ask them to write an article about his circumstances. The conclusion was, "Johnny W. Smith had come to Vietnam to fight for the freedom of the South Vietnamese. While in Vietnam, he got involved in drugs, contracted sexual diseases, and suffered alcoholism. He did not save South Vietnam from communism, but at the last moment of his life, a young Vietnamese lady doctor has saved his soul."

Thanks to Johnny's description of what he viewed, from the countryside to the city, Anna had a better picture of Vietnam in the time of the war, when she was too young to know about its devastation. She hoped that she would have a chance to go back to Vietnam herself to find out what she wanted to know.

3

Though unable to save Johnny's life, Anna believed that God had affectionately taken his soul into his hands. She prayed for him whenever she remembered him, and never did his soul come back to her in any way, even in dreams. As far as Anna knew, Johnny was happy, in the presence of God, looking down on the earth with eyes full of love.

Confidence and joy returned strongly to Anna. She was not afraid of working with the vets anymore, and she perceived that most vets also seemed to treat her with more respect and sympathy when she came to their room for routine checks. Most of the time she tried to finish her daily checking and examining quickly but thoroughly in order to have a little time for herself. Once in a while, she came into some interesting circumstances that caused her to linger with someone much longer. It happened that one morning, more than five weeks after the death of Johnny, Anna came to the bed he had occupied and saw a new patient. The man sat straight up, smiled, and then uttered a long phrase of which she did not understand a word. If he had not been smiling, Anna would have thought of him as another Vietnamese hater. Not knowing what he had said, she remained silent and stared at him.

He said, "Are you Korean?"

Anna knew then why she had not understood a word of what this man was saying. He had, in a friendly way, asked her something in Korean.

She answered him in a cordial voice, "No, I am not Korean. I am Dr. Anna Vu, who came from Vietnam, if it matters for you to know where I come from."

Anna realized that this was a Korean War vet, not a Vietnam vet as she often met. She had a sense that this man would give her a lot of chatting time. He looked old, ailing, and as if he suffered from liver problems—due to too much liquor, probably.

"You looked very much like a Korean girl to me. You are a beautiful lady, like most Korean women."

Anna knew she was facing a very clever and delicate patient who had probably spent quite a time in Korea. She thanked him for his compliment and then quietly found out who this man was.

His name was Kenneth D. Fulton, an army officer during the Korean War. He had been admitted through the emergency room the previous night. Having terminal liver cancer, he was hospitalized hoping for some treatment to prolong his life as long as possible.

Though he was in frequent pain, Ken loved to talk to Anna, probably due to the similarity between Anna and his long-past Asian girlfriends. Anna liked to have time with him, too, because she wanted him to talk about the Korean War, which she knew almost nothing about. Once her father had expressed his opinions that General MacArthur was very right when demanding that atomic bombs be dropped on China to end the war and destroy the communist regime, but thousands of soldiers had been killed at the Yalu River by his arrogance and fatal mistake of underestimating Chinese war power. This mistake was again repeated in Vietnam with General Westmoreland. In addition to the mistake of underestimating the enemies, MacArthur permitted a tragic mishap when more than three thousand Korean people—men, women, and children—were shot down by American troops when running away from the communist North.

Anna cared nothing about mistakes of General MacArthur, but the three thousand Koreans killed by Americans, the ones who came to protect them, made her uneasy. She had planned to ask her father but never had a chance. Now, Ken Fulton might tell her all about it.

Anna also observed that there were several similarities between Korea and Vietnam. Both have roughly the same shape as a letter S. Both were divided into two countries having the same political situations: the North for communism, and the South for democracy. The same group of countries supported the North in an effort to conquer the South and the same other group of nations assisted the South to defend its freedom.

The only important difference is that South Vietnam collapsed while South Korea still stays strong, both militarily and economically, and is still defended by the United States. At first, Anna thought that it could be disturbing for Ken to talk about the war again, but actually, he loved to bring up memories of what he knew and of his exploits during the time he served in the Korean War.

On several occasions, he brought up the horrible scenes caused by the war: soldiers and civilians blown into pieces by bombs, artillery, missiles, grenades, and handguns of all kinds; his devastating retreat with the enemy close behind. Thousands and thousands of US troops and allies were killed in the battle to push the Chinese north of latitude 38 degrees and then by being pushed back by the Chinese. Ken elaborately recounted as many details as possible in each battle, but Anna was really interested in the circumstance in which thousands of civilian Koreans were killed by US troops.

Trying not to make it a big issue, Anna asked him about it one day.

"I do, I was there at the time of the killings," Ken answered immediately.

"Why? Do you know why?" Anna stuttered.

"Several times, enemy fighters came and mingled with the refugees. They carried with them deadly weapons and waited in the camps for the best time at night to attack our unsuspecting military unit. Also among the refugees were some who served as intelligence agents for the enemy. They would observe and report every move of the US and allied forces. To avoid danger for millions of soldiers, the US had no choice except to kill them all, whether communists or innocent refugees."

Ken stopped for a sip of water, then added, "That was the war. Sometimes we had to sacrifice some to save many."

Anna wondered about what Ken had just said. Was that really enough to justify such an extreme act by the US troops in the Korean War?

The next day, Anna avoided mentioning the war to Ken, concerning herself with his health, which appeared to be deteriorating gradually instead of improving. Ken seemed not to care much about his status. Anna gently reminded him of his situation and asked him about religion.

Perceiving what Anna was up to, he told her, "I know what you are thinking, my dear doctor. You are indeed a good doctor. You take care of your patient's body and worry for his life after death, making sure that if you are unable to cure him, God will then bring his soul to heaven. That is your task in this world, as you may claim. You want to know my beliefs, don't you? You need to know the belief I belong to in order to call in the right person to prepare me for the life beyond. Thank you for your concern. As for me, honestly, I am unable to tell you what religious denomination I belong to."

Judging that Ken refused to disclose his beliefs, Anna changed the course of conversation by asking him to talk about his life and relatives. Instead of giving the answers she expected, he asked her, "You are a Buddhist, aren't you?"

"No, I am Christian."

Her answer surprised him. "I thought most Asians were Buddhists." He paused for a few seconds, then announced, "I do not know whether I am a Christian or Buddhist or something else."

"Your assumption about Buddhism for Asians is the same as mine about Christianity for Caucasians like you," Anna told him. "It surprised me to hear that you do not know to what belief you belong, neither Christian nor Buddhist and not sure even about something else."

At first Anna expected to know all about the war in just a couple of visits. Now, in hearing what Ken disclosed, she anticipated that she would need much more time with him to know of the reasons for his special circumstances. As Anna had predicted, in subsequent visits Ken went on and on, telling Anna dramatic stories about his beliefs and traumatic events in his personal life.

> *I was born on a very big farm in rural Texas that my grandparents had bought and settled as neighbors to more than ten other German families. This group of farmers was very proud of its origin, of its religion, Baptist, and of being called "redneck." My grandfather died when my father had just finished high school, and his widowed wife stayed there with her two sons, my father and his younger brother. At nineteen years of age my father met*

my mother and married her. They had three children: my older brother, me, and my younger sister. As opposed to our father, who loved us too much, our mother hated us and looked at us as unwanted. She often sought me out for physical abuse by kicking, beating, and slapping. Then suddenly I developed an unknown disease that made my right leg weaker and gradually smaller so that I was unable to walk anymore.

Seeking treatment, my father brought me to a doctor. This doctor, after examining my leg, announced that my disease was incurable and I had to be in a wheelchair for the rest of my life. My father was so angry upon hearing that! He took me away from that physician to look for another one. He told me to believe in him and that he knew I would be able for sure to walk one day. My father did not want me to lose hope when telling me that, but looking at his face, I knew he was very worried and disappointed.

That night, I felt desperate, sad, lonely, and unable to sleep. And a thought crossed my mind: I would rather die young than grow up handicapped. I thought of suicide. But before deciding how to die, suddenly I remembered that I was a Christian and a hope for a miracle changed my intention of killing myself.

I turned to God. With difficulty I knelt, leaning on my bed, and began to pray. Actually, I just talked to God, because I did not know how to pray.

"Oh God, I do not need to tell you my problem, because you already know. The doctor cannot fix it, but I know you can. If you do not want to do it, then let me die. Amen."

Miraculously, after saying prayers, I had the impression that my leg would be fixed. Hope returned and I could sleep peacefully *through the night. I kept praying for two weeks, but my situation had not improved. I stayed very calm, though, thinking that it was not the time yet.*

Seeing my good mood on my face, my father decided to bring me back to the church on Sunday, for we had been absent from the church services for several weeks. I wanted to go to church, too, because it would be better, as I thought, to pray to God at God's house.

On that fateful Sunday, after the services of the church, my father pushed me in my wheelchair to meet the pastor and to tell him the reasons for our long absence. Without paying attention to a word of my father, just looking at my leg and wheelchair, the pastor said aloud for everyone around to hear, "You are a sinner and being condemned by God for some grave sins that you have committed. You should stay away from my church and stay home to repent for your wrongdoings."

Though young, I was stunned when hearing what the pastor had said, and my father was furious. He grabbed my hand and gathered the rest of our family. We left the church in anger. Never did we return to that church and even avoided passing by it.

The incident at the church destroyed my trust in pastors as well as their teaching from the Bible. I sought to read the Bible myself at home and continued my nightly praying. One problem in my reading the Bible was that the more I read, the more confusion I had. There were so many issues that were not understandable or were unreasonable that I wanted to ask someone for answers.

One evening when just kneeling down, I heard some voice calling my name. I did not know where the voice came from. It seemed from outside, or from above, or in my head. At the second call, I thought it came from my father outside. I reached to open the door to answer him, "Dad, why are you calling me?"

I got no reply. I looked around and saw no one.

I came back to pray again and my name was called again.

I knew without a doubt in my mind that it was God who had been calling me. I followed the way in the Bible to answer, "Here I am, Lord."

That was it for the night. I waited and waited, and God did not call me nor send any signal that he was there. But I knew my disease would be cured.

From this time on, God often came to me in different ways: one time I might feel his presence; the next I might hear his voice in my head. Over time, I really believed in stories of miracles or of those who claimed seeing or talking to God. Previously, I did not believe God had ever really called Abraham until I myself heard him calling my name.

Only three days after I heard the call from God, someone referred my father to Dr. Richard Brawn, a brilliant foot doctor. I was brought to Dr. Brawn in my wheelchair. After asking questions and looking at the bruises on my body, Dr. Brawn announced that I had contracted Perthes disease. He then went on to explain Perthes. According to Dr. Brawn, something had hit my hip. As a result of the strong blow, blood had stopped circulating properly around the hip and down the leg. The blocked blood flow results in the leg getting weaker and gradually smaller. In order to cure Perthes, the patient has to be out of the wheelchair and use only crutches. With crutches to ease the pressure on the hip, reinforced by medicine to cure the wounded hip, the blood would flow again and the leg would gradually return to normal. It would take quite awhile to heal.

My father knew who had hit me and with what: My mother had usually beaten me with a baseball bat.

My father was so glad to know the cause of my disease and how to cure it. He embraced me and in an emotional voice he uttered, "I told you, do you remember, that you would walk one day. Didn't I?"

As for me, I knew it was the work of God that was going to cure me. He used time to test my patience and look for Dr. Brawn.

The discovery of Perthes brought two important impacts on my life.

The first one was the divorce of my parents. In order to protect his children from being abused by my mother, my father had to sacrifice his marriage. Ironically, she was happy to leave the farm, her children, and her husband to go with another man in the far city.

The second one was that I believed in the power of prayer. My belief in God was strengthened. This God is the one who had called me. This God has love for everyone, calls and listens to everyone in this world and others. He is not like the God described by some religious denominations.

Miraculously, my foot got better day by day and I was able to walk without crutches. My father was happy to see my health improving. In order to thank God for answering his prayers, he took and registered us with a Methodist church led *by a young pastor who was viewed by my father as very nice and understanding.*

At this new church, after each service on Sunday, I loved to stay to talk to the pastor. I found this a good opportunity to bring up the issues in the Bible that I considered unreasonable. At first, the pastor had tried to listen to me patiently. Gradually, he became uncomfortable and restless with what I asked, and his answers even gave me more confusion rather than understanding.

Then it happened again that one Sunday he waited for me at the church door, and instead of welcoming me into the house of God, with a low voice just for me to hear, he told me, "You should not come to this church anymore. You are not welcome here."

When turning away from me, he changed his mood from exasperated and cranky to smiling to greet other churchgoers.

My father took me home. That night, I was crying in my room for being rejected again by the church. It had been a long time since I had cried; the last time was when my mother hit me and accused me of stealing her money that she had never lost. My father did not ask me why I was driven out of the church. He might have gone back to confront the pastor to know the reason, but he never told or blamed me for anything. He consoled and covered me with love and affection. He wanted me to forget about churches and give all my attention to education.

Though devastated, I fared well in school, probably because of my father's encouragement and care. I invested my total time and energy in school and forgot about everything else. My foot got better and better and came to be completely healed. I was happy and confident of my bright future.

I graduated in the top ten of my class and prepared to go to college as my father got a job in the city. He moved out and took with him my younger sister. Being with my grandmother for a while and then with support from my father and grandmother, I went to college and majored in chemistry. My father died of liver cancer three months before I graduated from college.

I joined the army, became an officer, and was sent to the Korean War.

Ken stopped. He closed his eyes for a minute, then opened them and looked at Anna. "You were too young to know anything about the Vietnam War, weren't you?"

"I was old enough to know about fear and terror, dead and wounded, and bodies blown to pieces by missiles or artillery or mines, but too young to know how much Vietnamese people had suffered."

"By knowing about the war, I meant the nature of it," Ken said. "In the Korean War, the battles were very conventional. There were battlefronts that each side tried to push forward as far as possible. Moving the front back and forth would destroy thousands and thousands of lives each time. But the war in Vietnam had no clear-cut battlefronts. Battles in the Vietnam War were mostly about ambushes and counterambushes, attacks and counterattacks, mines, booby traps, and snipers. It was a guerrilla war and it was very tough to fight that kind of war, because the enemy knew where we were, but we did not know where they were hiding.

"Though different in nature, both wars had one thing in common: destruction. And of course people would suffer.

"I had been so proud being a soldier and fighting in the Korean

War. I would surmise that your father or relatives of yours might have fought in the Vietnam War, too. We have experienced more than what you have seen about destruction and suffering. In war, a soldier has to kill or be killed. He has to kill enemies to save other soldiers, friends, and allies. As a doctor, your main task is to save lives, but there are two tasks for a soldier: to kill a few to save many, or vice versa. That was why I chose to be a soldier instead of going to medical school."

Ken paused in order for Anna to digest what he had just said, and then he went on. "Those were my thoughts at the beginning and during the Korean War."

"And what about now?" Anna was anxious to know.

"After the war, back in the United States, in a car accident, my head hit something very hard, causing temporary memory loss. I was discharged from the military and I got married. Gradually my memory returned and I got a job as a lab technician for an oil company. After just six months, I had to give up the job, because my skin was allergic to most of the chemical substances in the lab. I went through some other odd jobs before I became a truck driver. I thought driving a big truck would give me peace for my troubled mind."

Ken's voice became weaker and more emotional. "The war's destruction and killing caused nightmare after nightmare. Marriage did not get rid of my bad dreams. I couldn't hold a steady job after being discharged from the military, and this devastated my daily life. I was away from home a lot, and before long, my wife's affair with a close friend was discovered and resulted in divorce. I moved away from Texas to Kansas City. All of these thoughts kept stirring my mind, and I had no peace.

I prayed to God for help, but this time he did not answer me. I thought there must be some reason that I didn't know. I did not blame God for all my mishaps, but I did not know what to do, either. I was dragging along, enduring year after year without hope or peace of mind. Then, while on a tour of Korea convened by a group of veterans, I happened to walk away from the group I was with that was visiting a certain city. I was wandering around and not having a clue where I was going. Before realizing it, I stepped into the front yard of a Buddhist temple. There was no one in sight. I walked into the temple when I saw the door open. Once inside of the temple, I had the feeling that I had been here before. But I had no memory of ever having come to this place. I sat down on a chair, and I felt completely at peace and happy. A melodious and religious music heard from far away seemed to call my soul to the heavenly realm.

Before long, an old monk dressed in brown appeared from the other end of the temple, walking toward me. Smiling and in a tone of empathy, he told me, "You have just walked through a threshold that permits you go from a troubled world to a peaceful one. I saw you coming, or rather I was expecting you to come, and I am here to welcome you."

The monk said his long name, and I could not remember it all. I just called him Monk Lee or Master Lee.

Master Lee spoke English fluently and there was no need for me to know where he had learned it. I told him my name and apologized for coming into the temple with no purpose in mind.

He smiled and told me, "You know well that everything has a reason, or cause and effect, don't you? Guided by instinct, a *thirsty animal runs to where there is water. In the same way, your troubled mind or soul seeks to find a peaceful place such as this. If you have no troubled mind, you would never have seen this temple."*

Hearing that, I was aware that this man knew a lot about me and that my Christian God had sent me to meet a Buddhist monk.

I then separated myself from the tour group to come stay at the temple. Returning to the temple the next day, I hoped to learn a lot from Master Lee. However, he denied any role as my master and stated that it was I who would be my own master. He was only the way, he said. I did not understand what he meant until later.

After seating me in a lotus position, he solemnly told me, "The core of human life is peace. In order to have peace, first of all one has to forget about everything around him, forget his own self. If he can forget completely his self, then nothing will be able to bother him, and he is at peace with himself, with others, and with God."

With that, Master Lee came to sit in a lotus position facing me about four yards away, eyes closed and hands clasped on his chest. He did not give me any order to do the same, but I realized that he wished me to follow his way to begin the journey of seeking peace.

For the first couple of hours, but like eternity to me, I had been struggling to keep my mind away from one event or the other in my past. I wished I had done them differently or regretted having done them. Then I heard some light, melodic sounds, a clear, distant, and holy music that seemed to come from a different world. This music lulled me into a dreamlike world in which I turned into an angel. I could fly from the earth into the immense universe. I forgot everything on earth, flying farther and farther, senseless of time and space.

I came to myself again suddenly when my mind was hit by an unhappy memory from the past. The music stopped. I opened my eyes to see that Master Lee was no longer there. I knew at once that my way to peace was blocked at some point. I looked around and had no idea what time it was at that moment. I looked through the door and saw Master Lee was waving, beckoning me to come out with him.

He congratulated me for a successful start and told me not to worry about blocking. Everyone must break through it to come to the end of the road, he told me. He saw that I was on the right way.

I stayed at the temple five more days to proceed with my meditative process.

Even though I had not quite completely forgotten my own self as Master Lee wanted me to, I sensed that I had changed, and I found peace of mind.

I came to see how important such peace was for each of us as human beings. It was so crucial that the angels sang to wish peace for the earth when the baby Jesus was born. And Jesus, too, had repeated and repeated peace again and again to his disciples whenever he met them. As for me, I had been on the long journey to look for peace. Now I had found it. I also found the truth about my problems: I do not need a teacher to show me how to solve them; it was I who had the cause and the effect of all, and at last, I had found my own self in a Buddhist temple.

Also from this peaceful place I was introduced to real Buddhism. To most Westerners and by definition, a religion is a belief—reverence for a supernatural power recognized as creator and governor of the universe. If based on that definition, then Buddhism or Taoism is not a religion, as Master Lee pointed out, but a way or road.

However, if we compare this meaning to the words, "I am the Way, the Truth, and the Life," as Jesus said, then Buddhism is not far from Christianity. Buddhism can be explained as the right Way that leads to the Truth about Life before and after death, in order to reach the Light, or Enlightenment.

As for Master Lee, he accepted only the role of a man at an intersection, waiting for a passing traveler in order to show him the Way that leads to Enlightenment or to God. Master Lee could contact God in his meditation, and he knew I could, too. He had said that there are a few people who could see or hear God, but in different ways. That was why there were many diverse religions, each describing God the way he appears to them and preaching different words of God as they had heard him. Unfortunately, each denomination perceives itself as superior to the others and claims it is the only one having heard the real words of God. Another matter of concern is that most religious denominations become more or less political organizations. Imagine how much influence religious denominations could have on an election for a democratic country and how powerful the denomination's leaders would be if it were a national religion. In many cases, people kill one another in the name of God. With Christianity, Jesus was judged and killed more for political reasons than religious ones.

In Buddhism, there are no leaders and churches, only quiet temples where one may find a monk waiting to show him the right way to follow as well as the wrong way to avoid.

Coming back to the United States, I saw myself as a Buddhist, though there was no ceremony or paper or witness or godfather, as Christians or others have. Besides, I still considered myself as Christian, also. This is why I do not know what denomination I belong to. As I thought of the two pastors who had condemned and rejected me, I harbored no more grudge against them, realizing that they might hear or explain God's words in a different way. I forgave them and I pray for them.

I kept going back to Korea once a year for my meditation processes until Master Lee passed away. In my dreams, I hear him saying that I had come to Korea to look for a war, but I found peace at last.

Once peace returned, so did the call of God. Right in this hospital, God called to tell me he would bring me home soon. Besides hearing God's calls, I happen to know that I am also a psychic, meaning that I can contact the dead as well. The first one was my father, who came to me and let me know that he was assigned as my guardian angel. I knew he was with me to look after me for only eight years; then he was gone. Once gone, he never contacted me at all again.

The second one involved my Korean girlfriend. Several years after my divorce, I met a Korean girl. She was brought to the USA through sponsorship of her older sister. The first time I visited her at her sister's home, she pointed at a picture and showed me who was who in her family. She said many good things about her father. He died soon after my first visit. The second time I returned to this house, her sister and her sister's husband, a white man, were also at home with her. I sat facing the man. While we were chatting, my girlfriend's father appeared. Without looking at either of his daughters, he stood behind the sister's husband. Just then I heard in my head that he wanted to thank this man for taking care of his daughters. He disappeared right after his last word. I told the girl what had happened and asked her to tell her brother in-law."

As if reaching the conclusion of his long life story, Ken came back to his reality by saying, "At almost the end of my bodily life, I realize it is difficult to know the difference between right and wrong, between harmful and favorable. Without the abuse from my mother and the condemnation from the first pastor, I would never have heard from God; without denial from the second pastor, my eyes would never have been opened to the different religions of the world. Now that I have heard God and seen or contacted the souls of the departed, I have no fear of dying, for the truth is that everyone must die anyway.

"You have asked me about my belief. I do not need anyone to guide me into the other world. Neither does someone need to talk with me about it. There are not many days left for me in this world. I am glad to go. However, I wish to see my mother to tell her that I have forgiven her and thank her for her abuse. It was her abuse of me that brought my soul closer to God. She may be among the ones who come to help and take me away."

CHAPTER 4
JOURNEY TO THE PAST

I

Anna was not at Ken's deathbed, but she had confidence that there would be a smile on his face as he left this world. The encounter with Ken and his dramatic life story gave her a lot to think and learn about. This was the first time she ran across a patient who had no fear of dying, unlike most—including herself. She reasoned that the fear of death could originate from two sources: fear of an unknown, mystical realm pictured differently by each belief or philosophy, and fear of being in the eternal fires of hell. This accounted for what someone termed the "scare tactic," which imprinted in people's minds that they had been born with sin and were living as sinners. Even after making confession, repenting, and asking for forgiveness, no one could be certain that all his sins had been absolved before dying. From Ken's messages to her, Anna had come to acknowledge three important precepts:

1. There is only one God, though there are many different denominations or beliefs.

2. God is love and acceptance.

3. The fear of death and the thought of ourselves as sinners are baseless. One should think of dying as coming back to God.

Anna took Ken's lessons very seriously. As a result, she thought she would act differently in dealing with dying patients.

Rather than diminishing her standing, the stories of Johnny and Ken made Anna somewhat renowned among doctors in Kansas City. Dr. Gerald D. Henson, the president of a medical charity association, called Anna and asked her to help the association with a mission to Vietnam, because Anna had the qualifications of both being a doctor and speaking the language. Dr. Henson went on to praise her and the Vietnamese people as brave, hardworking, and intelligent. He added that this would be a good opportunity for Anna to go back home.

Anna felt for the first time in her life a sense of pride as a Vietnamese. She humbly told Dr. Henson that she was an American now and that the United States of America was also her country. She happened to be born in Vietnam, but fate and the war had changed her from Vietnamese into American. Any event that caused bad or good to happen in Vietnam had no effect on her and her family unless it also happened in the United States of America. She also politely expressed her confusion about which way she would head in going home: Vietnam or America? She had only seven and half years in Vietnam, during which her parents had brought her through many different war-torn places. Though very excited to go to Vietnam, Anna asked Dr. Henson to give her time to think it over, because she was at the busiest time of her internship.

The next day, Dr. Henson called her again to assure her there was no need to worry about permission. He would get it for her.

Actually, Anna had been longing for a trip back to Vietnam to seek more information about the war, because there had been so much controversy over the fateful events that had had such a great effect on her life and those of millions of other Vietnamese and Americans as well. From its onset to the end, the whole Vu clan had been fighting in this war and then been uprooted from its homeland. Even Anna was born at a moment when her father was engaged in a fierce battle and a man next to him was killed. This war had devastated so many families, but paradoxically it had brought her and many others to the land of opportunity, the United States.

She wanted to know the truth about the war because there was so much different and contradicting information. What she had learned from the US history books at school was not the same as what she heard from people who had fought in the war. She had been diligently collecting information about the Vietnam War from many documents and sources, but she wanted to go back to the place where the war had happened, hoping to gain a better knowledge of it.

There were several other reasons Anna wanted to go to Vietnam. First, she wanted to visit the native village of the Vu clan. Her grandparents and parents would have loved to return just once to this place that they always described as beautiful. Second, she wanted to know about life under the communist regime. Why had her grandfather and father been against the communist government of Vietnam from its onset? Why had so many Vietnamese tried to escape the regime when the war was ending?

Next, Anna wondered: Why was it so important and urgent for the United States to decide to go into the war? Why did they choose to send armed forces to Vietnam? And then, why did they get out? She wondered why her father had not been happy with Americans and was still embittered toward them in many ways.

Forced out of Vietnam at almost nine years old, Anna was too young to know anything at all about the whole situation. There were many different opinions about the war: Some said the communist Vietnamese were winners and the United States the loser. Others said the US troops were neither defeated nor won—they just abandoned Vietnam. What Anna knew for sure was that the Vietnamese people were the losers and that the Republic of South Vietnam was destroyed by both friends and enemies. And the whole of Vietnam was now ruled by the dictatorship of a communist regime.

There were many other questions she wanted answers to: Why had she had been brought to the United States? Why were there Vietnamese in America and all over the world? What was the real purpose of the Vietnam War? Going to Vietnam would be a golden opportunity to find out many things she wanted to know. She would have a unique opportunity to visit the village of her paternal ancestry, and she especially wanted to see places connected to her early life, where she, as a young girl, along with her brothers and sister, experienced so many terrified moments. She had never forgotten the chaotic moments at the gate of the naval base when she and her siblings were all crawling over the ground as shooting and bomb explosions surrounded them on the day they escaped Vietnam.

It had been twenty years since the night her father brought her to a ship to escape the advancing force of the communists. At eight and a half years old, she had not known much about Vietnamese culture, and she still didn't. She wondered whether people were the same as before she left or different. Would they treat her nicely or look at her with hostility? All Vietnamese living abroad had said that it was necessary to be alert at all times once setting foot back in Vietnam.

Anna was going to meet with the communist officials and bring medicines and equipment to help them. She was going to see the country where she was born. She had lived there only a very short time, but it was her native country anyway. Her motive was to help poor Vietnamese, not communists. Apart from medicines and equipment, she would bring friendship, compassion, and love for the suffering people of a country that had been devastated by a very long war.

She hoped to have a chance to do something that her grandfather, before passing away, had bid one of his children or grandchildren to do. Just two days before dying, her grandfather had collected his strength to tell every member of the family that he had some unfinished business at his native village in North Vietnam. He had wished that he could come back himself to resolve what still nagged at him all the time, but he was unable to do it. He determined to reveal his secret, hoping that someone in the family could do it for him.

At the onset of the revolution for Vietnamese independence in 1945, he had joined an organization opposed to Ho Chi Minh when he discovered that Ho Chi Minh and his party were communists, not patriots. Before being arrested by the communists, he grabbed all his important documents, including the list of people in his networking group, sneaked into the village church, and put everything under a heavy statue at the highest place in the church.

He wanted his sons or grandchildren to try to recover these documents if possible, to avoid danger for the people on the list or their children. He had then drawn a map to indicate the exact position of the statue, hoping that his concealed information was still undisturbed.

The room was very quiet after he finished his story and request. Anna was the first person among those present to announce that she would recover these documents if the situation permitted. Her grandfather heaved a sigh. He seemed not very confident in a female voice to finish this job. But then he smiled and reached out for her hand, squeezing it lightly to express his thanks.

No one in Anna's family had ever gone back to Vietnam, especially North Vietnam, where Anna's father had been condemned to death in absentia in 1954, after he had moved safely to the South. By chance or fate, Anna would be the first in the family to go back since the United States lifted the sanction against travel to Vietnam and the Vietnamese government initiated an open policy to invite foreign investment.

In preparation for the trip, Anna took time to dig up more information about Vietnam and the Vietnam War. She also called her father to tell him of the coming trip and to ask for any advice he could give to her before going. Was there anything about the Vietnam War he wanted to remind her about?

Her father answered that he had nothing to tell her about the war, because it took so much time and caused so much pain to talk about it. It would be more truthful if she would see things for herself, both in the United States and in Vietnam, he told her. The Vietnam War was a strange one, so strange that generation after generation of American and Vietnamese people do not know what the war was about, he said. He added, however, that there was nothing for her to be afraid of. In reality, the United States had helped the North Vietnamese communists by transforming their South Vietnamese government ally into a puppet during the war. And there were many American celebrities who went to North Vietnam to praise the communists as heroes or patriots during the war and also to condemn South Vietnam's soldiers as killers and oppressors. Besides, Vietnam was one of the few countries that turned to loving its enemies after a fierce war. If she went along in a group of famous American doctors like this medical charity organization, the Vietnamese communist government would reserve its special treatment for the group and for her as well, he said.

Scheduled preparations for the trip to Vietnam went smoothly and as planned: money, permission for her leave of absence, passports, equipment, and medicines for distribution were all in place. Just the cost of the medicine alone had totaled up to $7 million.

One day before her departure, Anna went to her grandparents' grave and told them that she was going to Vietnam and that she would get to that church to retrieve the documents that her grandfather had hidden there.

It took almost twenty-four hours to go from Kansas City to Hanoi, the capital of Vietnam, a country formerly hostile to the United States of America. The goal of the medical team's mission was to bring humanitarian aid and friendship to a country that was once an enemy of the United States. To Anna, it was also a long-dreamed-of journey back to her origins.

Upon arrival, the twelve people in the team felt more excited than tired when they were invited to sit in the reception room of a government building. They were welcomed by Mrs. Binh, a vice prime minister of the Vietnamese government. Anna was chosen to give a speech of greeting, and she did it totally in Vietnamese, which surprised all the Vietnamese who came to receive them. Anna immediately gained the sympathy of many of the communist officials, and Mrs. Binh would later invite Anna to return to her native land and help in rebuilding Vietnam as a whole, without respect to whether a particular area had previously been communist or democratic. Anna politely said to Mrs. Binh that she would consider her request and inform Mrs. Binh of her intentions at a later time.

The team began working the next day by distributing medicines and equipment to each hospital in the capital and its surroundings. Besides filling the role of interpreter, Anna gathered young Vietnamese doctors to give them instructions about how to use the medicines and operate the equipment. Sometimes she also had to play the role of a diplomat between the Americans and Vietnamese officials. This caused her to think sometimes that the team actually came to Vietnam with a goal that was more political than humanitarian.

After three days of working in and visiting all the hospitals of the capital, Anna requested a day of personal leave to pay a visit to her relatives in Hanoi, while the other members of the team went on a guided sightseeing tour around the capital of Vietnam—including, of course, the mausoleum of their supreme leader, Ho Chi Minh.

Before going to Vietnam, Anna had made contact with a family of close relatives of her father; some of them lived in the capital, and some resided in his native village. With two trustworthy young men and a rented car, Anna headed straight to the village where her grandparents were born.

It took one and a half hours to travel the sixty-five miles from the capital to the village. She asked them to drive her right to the church in the village, pretending that she needed to pray first. Anna was in luck: the church door was open. Locating the position of the statue from the map described by her grandfather, she followed her guide to the indicated place. When the statue was lifted a foot off the ground, Anna extended her trembling hand to grab whatever was beneath. But when she opened the hand, all she grasped was dust and crumbs of paper, nothing else. She and her guide hurried away from the statue, took a look all around inside the church, and walked back outside before her traveling companions came to check on her.

She was sure that nobody had been up to the statue and lifted it up, and she was happy that the task had been completed quickly, causing no suspicion with the local authorities.

Standing outside of the church where her grandparents and father had been baptized, Anna tried to register as many details as possible of this place so full of their memories. She then identified two small brick houses, located on opposite sides of the rear of the church, the site of a horrible story from her grandfather about the deaths of thousands of children during the famine cause by the Japanese during World War II.

This story of her grandfather's was known by very few people in the rest of the world. When fuel and charcoal ran out, the occupying

Japanese had confiscated most of the rice, the main source of food for Vietnamese, to use to distill fuel for operating their locomotives. As a result, more than half population of this village—along with almost three million other Vietnamese—died of starvation. Now Anna was standing at the very site, remembering her grandfather's mournful narration.

> Beginning in mid-March of 1945, people ran out of food. There were beggars everywhere. With ruffled hair and ragged, torn, dirty clothes, they were trudging drearily in groups of two, three, four, or five and could be found on every corner of the village. Some had children, some didn't. Their looming eyes and fleshless cheeks were deeply hollow on deadly pale, gaunt, and dismal faces. They would sit at every crossroad, with difficulty stretching out their scrawny, dirty hands, asking for charity. They were hardly human beings, just lanky skeletons wrapped in wrinkled skin, hanging loosely on their bony legs, drifting from one place to the other.
>
> Children from ages two to seven were abandoned everywhere. Running back and forth, they kept crying and calling desperately for their parents in hoarse voices: "Mommy, Daddy . . ." They held their dirty hands tightly together, and their gaunt faces were covered with tears and dirt. Their parents were nowhere to be seen. There was no pity for abandoned children, though hopeless parents would leave them someplace, hoping that someone would pick them up and feed them. Wiping their tears as they did so, these parents thought that their children might have some chance of survival if they did this. These poor, hungry, and skinny children were found in various places: some in the middle of a

bazaar, some in Buddhist temples, some at crossroads, and many in the Catholic churchyard. The children wore torn clothes or no clothes at all. Their legs, arms, and bodies were skin and bone. Their chests revealed each rib. Their teeth and jaws stretched from hollow cheekbones. Their eyes, deep in the cavities of their faces, looked vainly in the direction their parents had gone, anxiously hoping for their return. Some of them kept calling for their parents with hoarse voices; some walked back and forth impatiently; some just sat silently on the ground not caring to even brush away the flies on their eyes and mouth. All of them protested strongly when being taken away. They insisted on staying at the spot, since their parents had promised to return and bring them food.

In this village, all children found were brought to two small, thirty-by-twenty-foot brick houses at the rear of the church, built for activities of the church associations and also as schoolhouses for parish children. There were no bathrooms, lights, or running water inside, and no one looked after the children.

Soon these buildings reeked with urine, excrement, and death.

For days and nights, children would cry for their parents and for food and water, until their last strength was gone. Once a day, the church attendant would come to clean up as much as he could and gather the dead children. Tying them in bundles of six to ten, he would carry them on either end of a balanced pole for burial in the field.

Once the dead children were picked up and buried, two nuns, one for each house, would come with a pail of water and a compressed rice ball. Each child was given a cup of water and a thin slice from the rice ball. That was their ration for twenty-four hours. The slice of rice became thinner and thinner because of the increasing number of abandoned children each day. Due to starvation, the children's eyes became blank and lifeless. They did not know who they were or who their parents were. There was no more mercy for children from the villagers, for they were not sure how many of themselves would survive.

There were twelve people in the family of Anna's grandparents during the famine. They had gone for more than fifteen days without any food at all. Miraculously, they pulled themselves through until the new rice crop came. They survived but were severely malnourished for a long period of time, and two young members of the family, an aunt and an uncle of Anna, died two months later.

Anna walked to one of the houses; it looked so lonely in the light of the morning. The door was locked. She looked through the bars of the window and saw some scattered chairs placed on the concrete floor and along the mortar walls. It was dark inside, revealing no details to commemorate the deaths of hundreds of children fifty years before.

At that moment two ladies about Anna's age passed by. They looked at her with puzzled expressions. Nobody knew who she was or where she came from, and Anna did not introduce herself to anyone. She was only a stranger, and all the villagers were strangers to her as well. They might not even remember who her father was. But then she considered the possibility that the people who had tortured her grandfather or condemned her father to death in absentia might have already passed away or left the village to earn a better living elsewhere. Perhaps there would be no more hatred, no more vengeance. Like the hidden documents of her grandfather, perhaps everything in the past had turned into dust or been forgotten.

She took some time to walk around the village. It did not appear as beautiful as her grandmother had described; it was unlike anything Anna had imagined while listening to her stories. The river that wrapped around the village had been filled up. The banyan tree at the entrance of the village had been cut down. The front yard of each house was being used as a place to germinate rice. No flute melodies came from the blue skies; no warm, low sound of a bell echoed from the pagodas hidden behind giant trees. The house where her father had lived had been dismantled and the land distributed to others in the village.

There were no children running around; the whole village seemed asleep. Anna thought that if her father were here at this very moment, it would be exactly like Rip Van Winkle coming back to his village after a short sleep. A sad feeling overwhelmed her at the thought that the Vietnam War had begun from peaceful villages like this one and resulted in millions of people dead or uprooted.

Anna had a pleasant feeling of accomplishment. She had come to the place where several hundred years ago her only ancestor had survived the religious persecution of Vietnamese kings. And her beginnings were in this very village.

Anna studied the map to look for the house of a widow whose husband had been tortured to death while refusing to disclose the names of his colleagues who plotted against communism—one of whom was Anna's grandfather. She followed a small path leading to a very small cottage. One very old lady with wrinkled skin was sitting on the dirt floor, eating something that looked like rice and vegetables. She was very surprised and stopped eating at Anna's approach.

When Anna identified herself as the granddaughter of Chan Vu, the old lady stood frozen awhile, and then tears began to fill her eyes. She embraced Anna and shook uncontrollably with emotion.

She murmured, "I thought I would never hear from your grandfather for the rest of my life."

Anna told the old woman that she knew everything from her grandfather about her husband's death. Hiding her grandfather's death, she then told the old lady, "My grandfather would like to know about you, whether you are healthy or not, how you and others have been living since he left the village. He seemed very concerned about your circumstances; what difficulties and troubles have you endured?"

"Tell him that I had some problems at first," the old lady replied. "My house was searched again and again, and when nothing was found after my husband's death, they left me alone. Then with time passing on, the whole world forgot who I was or whether I was living or dead."

Listening to the old lady, Anna became jittery, looking around anxiously. The old lady assured her that there was nothing to worry about because nobody knew the secret activities of the former days that Anna's grandfather and her husband had been engaged in. Anna instantly thought of the stack of documents her grandfather hid under the statue and wondered how many people would have been killed if it had been found in 1945.

Her thoughts were interrupted by the old lady. "Tell your grandpa that in the episode of the land-reform movement in 1956, five men were shot and six others were taken away from home at night to be buried alive. Among them, only one happened to be your grandfather's comrade. But he was shot for being richer than other people in the village, not for politics. The authorities denied any involvement in the act. If your grandpa and your father had stayed at this village, both of them would have either been shot or buried alive.

"No one knows how many people were shot or buried alive in the countryside of North Vietnam during this time. There are so many things I want to tell your grandpa, but it seems that you do not have time to be here any longer. Just tell him that I am still surviving, though through so many difficulties and dangers. I wish he could return to this village one day, just one time to see how things have changed. Everything has been turned upside down. Also tell him that I am living in a society where no one has belief in God or fear of him, so any crime could take place at any moment."

Anna gave the old lady some money and hurried back to the people who were waiting for her at the church.

On the road, Anna reflected on what the old lady had revealed and came to realize that the Vietnam War had really begun from this very faraway village a long time ago. Its victims were the ones who died of starvation, were shot, or were buried alive.

On the way to the village, Anna had not paid any attention to the passing scenery because of her anxiety about retrieving her grandfather's documents, but on the return trip, she observed people still cultivating the land with primitive tools. Ploughs were pulled by water buffaloes or by men. Sometimes, both parents dragged the harrow while the son of ten or eleven years of age held it from behind. All along the way, Anna only saw one tractor. She would later learn that the tractor tires were too expensive for most to buy.

2

Anna came back to Hanoi to have dinner with some high-ranking communist government officials as anticipated, and she was relieved that no one ever questioned where she had been.

The work of the team progressed as planned: four days they worked in the North, and three days they worked in the center of the country. Leaving central Vietnam, the team stopped in Saigon, or Ho Chi Minh City as it was now called, for four days. The hotel that the team stayed in was not far from the house where Anna's parents had lived before 1975. On her first afternoon there, she called a taxi to take her to the house.

Twenty years had gone by since she had left this place. All the neighborhood surroundings looked the same. She expected that she might meet people she knew, but she saw no one familiar. Most doors were closed and people stayed inside, even children. She noticed that everything had stayed the same except that the milky-fruit tree in front of her house had disappeared. A light feeling of nostalgia stirred in Anna, and she really wanted to go inside her house to relive the days of her childhood.

She knocked at the door. She knocked and knocked several times, but nobody came to the door. She waited for a few more minutes. Then she saw a lady about forty years old open the window, pull the curtain to one side, put her face between the window bars and ask, "Can I help you?"

Anna identified herself as a daughter of a former owner of this house and asked if she could come inside to remind herself of living in this house for more than six years as a child.

The lady did not tell her yes or no; she just pulled back the curtain, shut the window firmly, and walked away.

Nonchalantly, Anna walked back to her taxi and headed back to the hotel. But for the rest of that evening, she felt as if the memories of her young past had been stolen. She had lived at this house for less than six years, but she began to understand why her grandparents and father had wanted so much to revisit their native village. They had been born and raised during the historical events of the village and country that they loved for so long. She now shared with them the sorrow of being denounced by people of her own native country.

On their third day in South Vietnam, Anna wanted to visit Saigon, the capital of the South Vietnamese government before 1975, now renamed Ho Chi Minh City. From their hotel, she sneaked away from the team and went downtown by herself, dressing like any other girl of the city.

There were so many motorcycles and too many people. Later she found out that the city was so crowded because people escaping from the New Economic Area were forced to move there, even though they had little on which to survive. Beggars and peddlers were everywhere. Anna was stopped again and again and asked to buy almost everything. She wanted to buy several items to help them, but she knew she would be unable to carry it back to the United States.

Feeling tired, she came to an ice cream booth and planned to have some ice cream and relax awhile. Just as she sat down, several young ladies rushed in to invite her to buy lottery tickets. She refused them all. Then suddenly one lady about her age grabbed her and uttered her name: "Is it you, Anna?"

Anna did not recognize her. The lady added, "I am Hong, your classmate at Regina Pacis School. You may not remember me, but I do recognize you."

Hong put her lottery tickets back in her purse and assured Anna that she had a very good memory and a knack for remembering even people that she had only met once.

Anna did not remember the other lady at first, but the name Hong reminded her of something. Grabbing the lady's hand, Anna told her, "I remember you now. You were the oldest student and also the earliest to leave Regina Pacis that school year."

Anna asked Hong to have ice cream, and after a long conversation, she revealed to Hong that she had come from the United States.

That evening, Anna again evaded the team to meet Hong at a restaurant, hoping to learn more about what had happened in Vietnam right after the end of the war.

They chose a seat at the far corner of the restaurant to avoid being overheard. Looking at her friend and with a voice full of emotion, Anna asked, "Why did you leave school in such a hurry that year?"

"My father was wounded and hospitalized. My mother wanted me to quit school for a while."

"Tell me about your life after the end of the war," demanded Anna. "What was going on with your family and with the general public?"

Hong then confided in her friend all the calamities of her family.

After April 30, 1975, the Vietnam War might have been over for people like you, but those of us who stayed behind had to fight another war, the war of survival. First, even before the end of the war, there were millions of handicapped men and women like my father, who had lost one or more parts of their body while fighting for the cause of South Vietnam but were dismissed from the fighting force. Before 1975, they had been living on a humble pension to support themselves and their family. Right after 1975, that small source of income was cut off. They and their children could not get a job, because they could not hide the evidence that they had sacrificed for the enemy. Along with other millions of children of the dead soldiers, children who were half American and half Vietnamese, and children of the handicapped, all became unwanted and a burden for the new regime.

However, my father was not ashamed of his handicap. He was proud and made known to everyone that he was one of the wounded soldiers of the South Vietnamese Army, knowing that he could not hide it. He and his children have paid the dear price for his pride. Whenever asked how he lost his leg, he always proudly answered that he had been in battle as an officer of South Vietnam. That made the local communist officials mad. They arrested and imprisoned him along with other Vietnamese officers.

After about three years, he was released from the prison, or "reeducational camp" as it was called by the communist regime. He and his children were forced to move to the area that the government called the New Economic Area. Our house was confiscated. Hundreds of thousands of people like us were brought here against our will. The place was bare, not even a single tree around. I was told that this place had been a heavy dump site of Agent Orange during the war, and the new regime wanted us to come here to cultivate the land. Trees and animals could not live here, so how could we? The rulers wanted us dead, for we would die either by starvation or from cancer caused by Agent Orange. And this was the way for them to test this substance. The air we *breathe, the water we drink, and the food we eat all are contaminated with Agent Orange. I do not know how many people like us have contracted cancer; it could be just a matter of time. Some American soldiers worried about their health when they just sat on the airplanes and pressed the button to dump the substance. But at this moment, there were millions of South Vietnamese living in most of the places where tons of Agent Orange had been sprayed. We know it is difficult to survive here, but we have no choice, trying to cultivate the land.*

"As for my family," Hong continued, "before we could plant anything, a tragedy took place: my older brother was killed when his hoe hit a mortar shell. His body was scattered all over the newly dug ground."

Hong stopped her narration to reach for a napkin to wipe her eyes, blurred with tears. She turned around to see if anyone was watching. She continued.

"There were so many accidents here of this sort every day. Realizing we were unable to survive in this area, my mother sneaked back to Saigon, where she found a cousin who could take her in. Her cousin and his family members planned to escape Vietnam by boat. He wanted my mother to take care of his house and return it to him in case his escape failed. If he succeeded, the house would belong to my family. His neighbors were some of the Northerners who came to the South in 1954. They are all anticommunists, and they covered for us. My mother had prayed for her cousin's success so that she could have the house and her family could come back to Saigon."

Again, some sort of emotion overtook her and made her unable to go on. Anna could feel something important about to be said. Finally, Hong went on.

"Anna, we have the house now. My mother has sent word to us to come back one by one to avoid being noticed. But her cousin's escape ended up in disaster. The Thai pirates stopped his boat, took all their possessions, killed all twenty-four men, including my mother's cousin, and kidnapped fourteen girls. Two of the girls were the daughters of my mother's cousin. The pirates brought these poor girls to sell. I am very sure at this moment, thousands of Vietnamese girls and women are forced to be prostitutes in Bangkok or some place else in Thailand.

"We own the house, but our luck was at the cost of the misfortune of our kind relatives. My cousin's wife and two young boys, along with the other survivors, made it to Indonesia. They were admitted into the United States very soon after their arrival to the refugee camps. I believe that for the rest of their life, the terrifying experiences at sea will never cease to haunt them."

Hong paused awhile. She seemed hesitant to say what she was thinking. "We have a corrupt government and a hopeless country. My parents want very much for their children to escape, but on one hand, we do not have money, and on the other, we are fearful of the pirates.

"I do not ask you for help. I just want to send word by you to whoever is still concerned about the plight of their combatants, including the American soldiers who had fought side by side with Vietnamese. Wounded soldiers like my father have no place in this society, not even with their children. They are also the bravest men in the old regime, but they have been forgotten or humiliated by the world. There are several Vietnam vets who have come back to Vietnam to meet with the communist soldiers at some places where they had been trying to kill one another. But none of them come back to meet their allies who were left behind and were tortured by enemies, men whose wives and children are lying in the slum and fighting for their survival, politically and economically as well.

"Anna, do you know how many Vietnamese officers and enlisted men died during the course of the Vietnam War? I am too young to know the exact number, but I could estimate about two million. Some of them were single, some married with children. When the war was over, their children had to fight another war, not the war of survival alone but also the war of the stigma on their father's body."

Anna's father would spend great efforts raising money in the United States of America to help wounded soldiers in Vietnam as Hong requested. Unfortunately Hong's father fell ill and died of cancer just two years later. His daughter argued that it was not the Agent Orange that killed her father, but the Vietnam War instead.

In Vietnam after the war, there were many other circumstances worse than that of Anna's friend that were unknown to the world. Anna promised herself that she would bring this issue to the public's attention, seeking help in the United States.

Anna trembled, imagining what life would be like for her and her whole family if her father had not escaped Vietnam on the last day of Saigon. Their situation would have been worse; her father would have been in prison for at least ten years. How would her family have survived without the money her mother had lost? She and her siblings might still be wandering around the New Economic Area or in some city, selling lottery tickets. There would have been no chance for her or her siblings to go to school at all here, but by going to America, she was able to become a medical doctor. Smiling bitterly and silently, she thought of the fate of human beings. The same war had shattered the life of one and given better opportunities to the other.

The next day Anna and some of the other doctors made visits to public hospitals in Saigon, according to the schedule. The purpose of the visit was to see how the team could help with medications and medical equipment and supplies in the future. At the same time, they also had the chance to see some patients. Anna was requested the most because she could speak the language. The patients asked her all kinds of questions about medicine and about life in America. During the visit, one of the old patients suddenly asked her, "Can I talk to you privately?"

Anna looked to see if anyone was around. She thought that the old patient wanted to complain about something. She seemed to acknowledge Anna's caution and said, "Do not worry. This only concerns matters of my family, and I want you to do me a big favor."

Anna sat down on a chair and was ready to listen to what the old patient wanted to say.

"I want you to look for my daughter in the USA."

"Looking for your daughter in the USA? Do you know the city and state where she is living?"

"No, I do not know where she is. The only thing I found out is that she is in the USA."

Anna asked, "How you know that your daughter is in the USA?"

"She sends me money sometimes but never reveals her address."

Anna shook her head and told her, "I cannot find her if I do not know where she is living."

The old lady persisted, "If you live in the USA then you can find her someday."

The lady showed Anna a picture of a very beautiful Vietnamese girl about twenty-two years old, and with a tone full of emotion she said, "This is my daughter, my only child. She disappeared and left behind all the people who had loved her so much. Now she is in the USA. Please find her and tell her that her father died and her sick mother, Minh Thu, wants to see her before she dies."

Thinking quickly, Anna knew that would be impossible to find the young lady. However, she asked the old patient why she disappeared, and the lady briefly told Anna, "Her name was Lan Huong, and Ho is the last name. We were a wealthy family and sent her to a famous school because she is the only child. Growing up, she married a man who also belonged to a rather rich family as well. The war cut off our sources of income and gradually we became poorer and poorer. Her husband worked for the South Vietnamese government and his salary later was not enough to support the whole big family. My daughter reluctantly went to work for an American organization to earn more money. She and her husband were very happy at the time. Then suddenly my daughter left her work, her husband, and parents without any word for anyone. Nobody knew where she was and why she ran away. At first we thought she was dead. Then suddenly after 1975, once in a while we received money from her, sent from the USA. She never wrote me any word or explained anything. That's all."

Anna said she would try to find the old lady's daughter, but she did not promise anything. She considered this story another feature of the Vietnam War: thousands of Vietnamese women had deserted their poor husbands to run after money, either with newly rich men or with foreigners. This Lan Huong could have been one of them.

3

Her doubt and pity from the hospital visit were quickly forgotten in the welcome the team received at the last hospital they were assigned to visit: the place where Anna was born in Can Tho, a capital of western Vietnam. The hospital staff stood in a line in front of the main door of the hospital to wait for the team. Before Anna's introduction to each member of the team, one man who identified himself as the executive director rushed to embrace her and called her a beloved daughter of the hospital. He then told everyone that he had received all the information about the team, including the fact that Anna was born at this very hospital twenty-eight years ago and that they were anxiously waiting for her as a member of their family. The director's statement made Anna happy though she knew it had been for political purposes rather than a real feeling for her. A quick sense of alert also warned her that if they knew all about her, they would know all about her father, their enemy who had fought against them and who had been stationed somewhere around here. After the affectionate welcome, Anna announced a laboratory project for the hospital, which was a plan to modernize it by supplying some important equipment.

The mission was done after only two days, and the whole team wrapped up to come back to Saigon before returning to the United States. When leaving Can Tho, Anna realized she was as indifferent as anyone else on the team. She did not have much feeling for the place where she had been born; she had spent only a couple of weeks of her life in this town. Nothing of this place was imprinted in her mind. She had envied her parents of their love for the place where they were born. But she came to this world in one place, Can Tho, and was brought along the paths of her father, who had been stationed in various places during the war. There was nothing beautiful or memorable for her in Vietnam, only terror, destruction, and worry. The war and hardship had robbed her of what should have been an innocent, golden time in her young life.

As the team left Vietnam, Anna's head was still full of questions: Am I going home to the United States from my birthplace, Vietnam? Who actually brought me to the United States—the American government, the communist regime, or the Vietnam War? What would have become of me if I had stayed in Vietnam?

By going to the United States, she became a medical doctor, and when returning to Vietnam, she was treated as an honorable person. Over time, she had changed from the daughter of an enemy to a faraway, praised patriot of the new regime.

On the long trip back to the United States, Anna had time to reflect on the journey and her days in Vietnam. She tended to believe that everything had a reason, and she now knew why she had been chosen to go to Vietnam. On the one hand, she was very pleased by what she had accomplished on the trip. On the other, she was unhappy to see Vietnam in such a hopeless situation. To her it seemed that a person should be delighted to visit his native country and proud of its prosperity, beauty, comfort, and freedom. However, Anna found none of these; there was no quality that Vietnam could be proud of.

After the trip from Vietnam and before resuming her work as an intern, Anna again came to her grandparents' tombs and told them, "Grandpa, you may know that I have just come back from where you were born, where you hid the papers. I saw none of your enemies. Your fear turned into dust in my hand. Now you can rest in peace."

She also called her father and reported on what she had seen and done.

Anna had three more days off before going back to work. She took time to write down her thoughts about her efforts to complete one of her goals in life: to seek the real truth about the Vietnam War. She wrote:

> *The leaders of the communist regime, from the very beginning, were not fighting for the independence of Vietnam. The announcement on the second of September 1946 by Mr. Ho was not a claim for independence of Vietnam; it was the announcement of the replacement of the French colonial state by a communist regime. From that time on, communism dragged Vietnam back to the feudal society of more than a hundred years before. It destroyed the rich and the landowners in order to establish a new caste of people who were richer and more powerful than the ones they aimed to eliminate.*
>
> *Without a connection there was no job, no matter what college degree a man had. The power passed down from generation to generation. The director father would create a director son. Everything was for sale for money or gold. Communism was dead. From the capital to the other cities and the countryside, people talked like communists, but in reality they did not act like communists nor practice communism. It was like capitalism but not real*

capitalism, either. There were no fixed laws anywhere. Laws were subject to change according to space and time, arbitrary depending on the level of importance. The communist cadres live in luxury while the majority of people are terribly poor. Vietnam might be the poorest country in the Asia.

Vietnam's economy was dead. Products from China are overwhelming the country, killing Vietnamese businesses. In politics, Chinese influence dominates both in the governmental and public areas. Actually, the Vietnamese communist officials have been the copycats of China. Most Vietnamese scholars worry that sooner or later, Vietnam will become little more than one of China's colonies. They warned the country by saying,

"To all beloved countrymen:

Do not be quick to amass wealth. If not America today, China will be tomorrow."

This warning quote was written in Vietnamese from someone who had secretly copied it for Anna.

Her visit to Vietnam was the last phase of Anna's quest to find out about the Vietnam War. After spending much time researching different documents and history books, after conducting interviews of both Vietnamese and Vietnam veterans, recalling the terrifying moments of her life, and reviewing the history of the Vu clan, Anna wrote her summary of the Vietnam War:

The Vietnam War has been considered the most unpopular and costly war in the US history, both in money and human lives. No one wants to talk about it now for fear of evoking the humiliation and shame. But the more people try to forget, the more they are reminded every day, because the names of more than 58,000 beloved soldiers are seen on the Vietnam Memorial wall every year. In reality, not many people know much about the Vietnam War.

When did it start and end? What was the purpose of the war? Who was the real winner and who the real loser?

The cause of the war might be considered to have originated from Christian missions in the early years of the sixteenth century. Hundred of thousands of people had converted to the new faith. The ensuing persecution of the Christians and European ministers were the excuse for the French to invade Vietnam, beginning in 1858. The Russian revolution in 1917 and the victory of Chinese communism in 1949 were also origins of the war. Communism took advantage of the class struggle to stir up the revolution in many poor countries, including Vietnam.

The Vietnam War would never have taken place if several circumstances had been different:

1. If the United States had dropped atomic bombs on China during the Korean War as suggested by General MacArthur, it would have destroyed the new communist regime there.

2. If Japan had not invaded China in World War II, the insurgent communists would have been completely destroyed by the government of the Republic of China.

3. The British and the United States of America did not assist the French with finances and weapons to destroy communism in Vietnam.

The Vietnam War actually started in most villages in North Vietnam before the French returned after World War II. The return of the French provided the communists with a cause to fight for. People like my grandfather faced a dilemma: either stay in the countryside to fight and be killed, or go to the cities with the French and be called traitors.

The fighting against communism had gone on for a long time before 3,500 US Marines landed in Vietnam on March 6, 1965. The number of US soldiers increased gradually, as demanded by the evolving situation, until there were more than a million. The goal of the US forces was to destroy every unit of the communists in the South to stop communism from spreading through the rest of Southeast Asia and then to the whole world. So, the real goal of the war was to break up the Communist Bloc and stop its expansion.

With their modern, powerful weapons and undefeated armed forces, the policymakers of the USA thought they could accomplish this goal in a few weeks. But they failed, because this war was very different from others. In this war, it was difficult to know who were enemies and who were friends; the powerful and modern weapons could not be used effectively, because the enemies were nowhere or everywhere.

In order to go on with the war, Vietnamese communists had to rely on heavy assistance from the Communist Bloc, mainly the Soviet Union and China. As the war dragged on, there was a struggle for leadership between Russia and China. With this crack in the Communist Bloc, the US government changed its strategy by sending President Nixon to meet with Chairman Mao Zedong in China on February 21, 1972. After three days of talking, both sides agreed on principles for ending the Vietnam War.

On February 25, 1972, the fate of South Vietnam had been decided. However, the fierce battles continued, and thousands of brave young men of both sides kept killing one another.

No one knew exactly what the leaders of the USA and China discussed. It seems likely that there may have been an agreement that if China helped the US forces to get out of Vietnam with honor, the USA would aid China's modernization as a nuclear power, helping both militarily and economically. There could have been more promises that China quickly accepted. These would be highly confidential documents that would never be revealed. What is known is that following the visit of President Nixon to China, there were mass demonstrations in the USA to protest the war and to demand the complete withdrawal of US troop from Vietnam as of August of 1972.

Following negotiation after negotiation, US troops began to be withdrawn from Vietnam, passing the responsibility of fighting the war to South Vietnam's army. March 29, 1973, was the day the last US troops left Vietnam.

Once US troops were out of Vietnam, the US Congress voted to cut off most of the aid to South Vietnam.

Through lack of weapons, supplies, and money, the South Vietnamese government collapsed by April 1975.

On the last day of the regime, more than a hundred thousand Vietnamese were able to obtain transportation to escape the country. The rest were captured and imprisoned.

The war appeared to end on April 30, 1975.

The whole world perceived that the USA had been defeated and pushed out of Vietnam. In the US, people called it an unpopular and dirty war and avoided talking about it. The US policymakers and government kept their lips tight, regardless of what the world was saying, because they did not want to anger either Russia or China.

However, no matter what people said, the USA won the war, rather than being defeated. The goal of the war was to stop communism from expending and then to destroy it. When this goal was attained, there was no need for the US troops to stay in Vietnam any longer. The new policy was concerned only with how to get the troops out with honor to end the war. The US government brought the troops back home because, thanks to the new dynamic set in motion between China and the Soviet Union, they were no longer needed, not because they were being pushed out. They set up a schedule to get their troops out without paying a bit of attention to the fate of South Vietnamese people.

The collapse of South Vietnam's government took place as anticipated, though it came sooner than the US policymakers expected.

The communist North successfully conquered the South and was declared the winner. The long, unpopular, and costly war had ended—for people in the United States. Most American people thought the US was defeated, but very few knew that actually communism would be the eventual loser. Indeed, the glory and greatness of the Vietnam War for the American government are far more sublime than that achieved in World War II. The leading forces of America had fought and destroyed Nazism and Fascism in World War II, ideologies that people in the rest of the world loathed. But very few realized that with the Vietnam War, American troops eventually saved the whole world from the most dangerous enemy of mankind, communism. Right after World War II, the mere sound of "communism" could cause hysterics in the US Congress. But just when the expansion of communism seemed unstoppable, the Vietnam War provided a wedge to crack the solidity of the Communist Bloc. As the Soviet Union used its puppet regime in North Vietnam against the democratic forces aiding South Vietnam, China chafed at Russian authority so close to its own borders. Chinese communist leaders declared that the Soviet Union, burdened by expensive adventures in Africa and Latin America, did not deserve that leadership. The ensuing struggle for leadership between the two communist giants was exacerbated when President Richard Nixon visited China in 1972. China denied the Soviets the ability to transport weapons to North Vietnam through China, citing security concerns. As the Chinese and the Soviets struggled over who would lead world communism, communist ideology developed even more fault lines. With the withdrawal of US forces from Vietnam and the North's conquest of the South, communism was transformed into something else. Now, people talked liked communists, but they did not live like communists anymore. The fracture in the Communist Bloc, followed by the loss of a cohesive communist ideology, led eventually to the collapse of the Soviet Union. So, by means of the Vietnam War, the US and her allies set the stage for victory in the Cold War.

 The real loser of the war was the country of Vietnam.

 After the war and under the new regime, the nation's moral base has been destroyed completely. People live under a corrupt and lawless government. Everything is for sale, and jobs require *connections more than knowledge or ability. In education, degrees and diplomas are given to anyone who can pay the set prices. Most of the people are very poor, while the Communist Party members are very rich. Crime is rampant, and no one trusts anyone. The most afflicted people are those who were soldiers or officials of the South Vietnamese government before 1975, the wounded, and the wives and children of the millions of unknown soldiers who gave the ultimate sacrifice in the war. Their misery after the war and under the communist regime is unimaginable.*

The worst thing about the war may have been part of the deal between Mao Zedong and Nixon: cheap Chinese products that suffocated much of the industry and economy of Vietnam, along with fruits and food for Vietnamese people contaminated with substances that cause cancer. Vietnam is a hopeless country.

These were the ideas about the Vietnam War that made sense to Anna. She felt very sad, but she knew there was nothing she could do to help her poor native country.

4

Now Anna knew why she had been chosen by fate to be in the veterans hospital to work with the vets, most of whom were Vietnam vets. Before coming back to work after her trip to Vietnam, she perceived that there were two things she must do. The first one would be to announce to the American people and the whole world that the US troops had in reality achieved the greatest victory in the Vietnam War. The second would be to reclaim the honor, pride, appreciation, and respect for the Vietnam vets and those who had sacrificed their lives or a part of their body in the war. They were the heroes of their country, not its humiliation. More than sixty thousand US soldiers, dead or missing, had sacrificed for the cause of freedom.

Anna remembered a day during her time in Vietnam, when the team was on its way to the South, when they were scheduled for a guided tour of some battlegrounds where fierce fighting had taken place. In one location, while the car slowly crawled along the rocky, narrow path to reach the hill that had been the center of a fierce battle between North Vietnamese communists and US Marines, dark clouds suddenly covered the sun. It became chillier and chillier as the car climbed up the hill. Everyone in the car, including the guide, became quiet, absorbed in his or her own thoughts.

The car stopped in front of a little hut built in front of a thick wood of firs and pines. The medical team got out and was led to the hut, which served as a temple. Inside, incense burned in a big china bowl; beside the bowl some artificial flowers stood in a plastic vase. It was in the afternoon, the sky was cloudy, and the atmosphere was gloomy. All was calm and silent. Not even the sound of birds could be heard outside, only the sorrowful sighing of someone in the team.

Anna suddenly had the feeling that the brave dead soldiers of both sides were still around and looking at her. When everyone was silent and busy imagining what might have been happening more than thirty years ago, at an unexpected instant, a sweet voice from one person in the team rose, reciting a poem written by Mary Elizabeth Frye and published by the US Navy in the 1930s. Time seemed frozen as the poem was recited:

Do not stand at my grave and weep,
I am not there—I do not sleep.
I am the thousand winds that blow,
I am the diamond glints in snow,
I am the sunlight on ripened grain,
I am the gentle autumn rain.
As you awake with morning's hush
I am the swift-up-flinging rush
Of quiet birds in circling flight.
I am the stars that shine at night.
Do not stand at my grave and cry,
I am not there—I did not die.

There was complete silence as the poem finished, except for the murmur from the pine trees. Anna would never forget that day.

And this was all Anna knew about the war, a fateful conflict in which so many people had died to destroy communism. It was also a war that brought Anna and millions of other Vietnamese to the United States and to other countries all over the world.

Anna knew her father, though grateful for being given refuge for himself and his family, still harbored a grudge against America. She called him and said, "From the standpoint of a Vietnamese before 1975, it is very true that the USA did not live up to her promise, that she betrayed and abandoned Vietnam. However, if you take the position of a US citizen, you would put US interests above everything. As a matter of fact, the US involvement in Vietnam was not in the interest of Vietnam, but that of the USA and the free world. We are now the citizens of the USA and no longer Vietnamese. We, as well as others, have to sacrifice something for the great cause of humanity."

CHAPTER 5
A JOURNEY OF SPIRITUAL ENCOUNTERS

I

Her two weeks of visiting Vietnam gave Anna more energy to come back to finish the first year and get ready to go into a new year of residency.

As the second year began, there were even more patients to care for—and more deaths. Some passed away peacefully, some with severe suffering, and some with great fear. Some patients Anna thought were dying revived after resuscitation.

Working regularly with patients, Anna heard stories concerning near-death experiences, or NDEs, but she did not give them much credence until the first month of her second year of internship. A Vietnam vet named Bill had been admitted into the hospital late one evening with kidney failure. Bill received an intravenous dye in preparation for an X-ray of his kidneys. Unfortunately, he was allergic to the dye; his body went into anaphylactic shock and his heart stopped.

Anna was busy with another patient at the far end of another building when she was paged to come to Bill's bedside. Six minutes elapsed before she could get there, but as soon as she arrived, she rushed immediately to resuscitate Bill. The entire team took turns with Anna to resuscitate him, but for at least one hour they were unsuccessful. Normally, the patient would be pronounced dead and the resuscitation would stop, but Anna felt a very strong urging to keep going and not give up on this patient. She believed Bill was too young to die. She instructed the nurses to go off protocol and gave him higher doses of ephedrine to revive his heart. And then, at the very moment even Anna was ready to give up, suddenly Bill's heart began beating, to the surprise of everyone.

His pulse was somewhat weak at first, but gradually strengthened and returned to a normal, regular rate. Anna was able to stabilize him and transfer him to the ICU for the night. Bill was still unconscious, but Anna, though exhausted, felt so delighted that for the first time in her life and by intuition she had saved a patient's life. She went back to her routine agenda and hoped there would be no more urgent calls for the night.

At about two a.m., the nurses called Anna again when she was about to take a short break. The nurse told her that Bill had awakened and pulled off all the tubes from himself, demanding to see the physician.

"Tell him," Anna told the duty nurse, "he does not need to see a doctor now, and I will come to check on him in the morning."

Two minutes later, the nurse called again, saying, "Bill seems to be stable, but he persists that there is something very important that he wants to talk to you about at once."

On the third call, the nurse said that she could not calm the patient down if he was denied seeing the Asian doctor he kept asking for.

"Asian doctor!?" Anna repeated. Maybe this was another patient like Johnny who hated Vietnamese, Anna thought. Maybe the nurse told him about Anna when he woke up. She was very sure that this patient was going to blame her and all Vietnamese for his sickness and prepared for what she had to do in dealing with him.

But in contrast to her expectation of encountering a mean and angry face, when she went to see Bill, she saw a calm and happy man who was waiting for her expectantly.

"I am Dr. Vu, the Asian one that you are insisting to talk to," Anna said and waited for his reaction.

For a long moment, the patient just smiled and stared at her without saying anything. Anna tried to remain calm but she felt uneasy. She pushed him for the answer. "What is so important that you need to talk to me immediately?"

"Thank you! Thank you, doctor," Bill said.

"You thank me for what?" Anna was puzzled.

Looking at her face from his bed and with a voice full of emotion, Bill said, "I wanted to see you and thank you right away for fear that I may not have a chance to meet you again. You have saved me from burning in the eternal fires of hell."

Anna and the others standing around had no clue what Bill was talking about. She looked at him, still puzzled, and tried to make sense of what he was saying. Anna's immediate reaction was that Bill was delusional. However, she was baffled about how he knew it was an Asian doctor who rescued him.

"Who told you that I was Asian?"

"Nobody told me anything," Bill protested, "I myself saw and heard everything you did as you gave orders to the others to keep trying to bring me back to life."

Anna was perplexed. How had Bill known she was there when his heart had already flatlined before her arrival? She had never met him, and she left him before he regained consciousness. How did he know she had given extra efforts to save him?

Bill's body was trembling, either with emotion or from the trauma he had just survived. After about three minutes to calm down, he then recounted to Anna what he had been through.

"I was lying on the table waiting for whatever would be needed for my kidney failure. When a nurse injected the dye into the IV for my X-rays, I felt immediate warmth, then hot, very hot. I tried to warn the nurse about this but felt myself getting sucked into a very dark place. Though it was very dark, I could perceive it as a long tunnel. At the end of the tunnel I was immersed in fire and intense heat. I experienced horrible pain and burning, and I screamed and screamed but no one came to my rescue. I continued to be burned until I was jolted by a sudden force that sucked me back through the same tunnel and sent me up above the bed where I looked down and saw multiple people trying to resuscitate me."

Bill paused and turned to look around his bed. He raised a hand and pointed his index finger at a corner of the bed and continued, "It was at that corner at the end of the bed that you stood and gave orders to the resuscitation team. I remembered what you said. You repeated again and again, 'Continue CPR. Don't stop, please. He is too young to die, for God's sake.' I saw the light blue color of the shirt you were wearing. Then I found myself getting heavier and heavier until I was back in my body, and then I found myself waking up in this ICU room.

"Recounting what had been occurring to me, I resolved that I was really dead and sent to hell. When my soul was sucked back and left floating a moment above the bed, I discerned the extra effort you put into my resuscitation that brought me out of the hell and back to life. My reason to meet you was just to thank you for saving me from a burning hell."

Anna had never believed in hell. She considered that most religions had created the concept of heaven to encourage followers to do the good deeds and that of hell to keep people from wrongdoing. Based on right and wrong, reward and punishment, heaven and hell had come to existence. However, right or wrong at one time may not be the same at another, the same for all groups of people, the same from one country to another, or even the same from one religious belief to another. During Anna's younger years, she had a strong belief that heaven was high above the sky among the beautiful clouds, where God lived in a white, glorious house at the center of a magnificent garden full of lush trees and fragrant, multicolored flowers. There was always music from the birds and the angels. Down far below the earth is the hell where Satan, devils, and wicked people live. But these ideas made no sense to her as an adult.

Anna had read about near-death experiences and had heard a lot of stories that she neither denied nor accepted. Her grandfather, in fact, reported on such an experience during her first year of medical school. He was hospitalized at Saint Joseph's for two days with kidney failure, among other problems, when his heartbeat became irregular and then stopped. After about thirty minutes, he responded to resuscitation efforts, regaining his heartbeats. Later, he recounted what he had undergone. "I was inside a tunnel where I felt warm and comfortable," he told them. "Faraway at one end of the tunnel, I saw bright light, a kind of light I loved to look at. At the moment I was close to the source of the light, I was pushed back and became myself again."

Anna was very sure that her grandfather had never read nor heard of any near-death experience before, yet his description of his journey was similar to most of the others she had heard, though quite simple: he went into a tunnel, saw the source of light, and returned to his body. He did not say anything about what he had seen, heard, or felt. He seemed happy afterward, and he died three weeks later.

Anna was confident that her grandfather had not simply made up the story, but she was also not convinced that he was really dead. She also perceived that in some cases of NDE, patients might not completely die; perhaps their heartbeats were so feeble as to be undetected by either machine or medical personnel.

But Bill, her own patient, had told her what he had experienced, whether she believed or not. Before, she had listened to stories of NDE very impersonally and indifferently, the same way someone might hear a news report about a fatal accident or see it on television. But this time, Bill's life was saved; she was deeply and personally involved. Bill's experience had not been much different from others', but she was perplexed by the fact that Bill had been sucked out from hell. He had also described very precisely the activities taking place around his unconscious body among the people who had helped resuscitate him. Anna wondered whether it was really possible that

Bill had been dead and his soul had actually left his body, gone to a burning place, and come back to see all the efforts to save him. She was not sure she really believed in what Bill had recounted, but she had to admit that Bill had described exactly what had been taking place while he was unconscious. What was it that had seen everything? His spirit, soul, or consciousness? Was this the same entity that Dr. Dexter described as invisible to our eyes, yet able to travel around to register what was happening around the unconscious body?

Before leaving him, Anna humbly told Bill that she was not the person who had saved him: God had done it. God had used her as an instrument in this process to fulfill his will. Besides, she was not the person he needed to talk to; the one he needed would be a chaplain.

Bill did not seem very pleased with what Anna told him. He looked straight at her, saying, "You and others may not believe me and ascribe whatever I experienced to hallucination, illusion, fascination, or fancy as you will, but I suffered in hell and thanks to you, I was released from it."

Anna calmed him down by saying, "Bill, I am very glad that you have this chance. There must be a purpose or reason that God would give you a second chance, and now it is up to you to find out what it is."

A few weeks after this incident, Bill came back to the hospital to thank Anna again, trying to find out whether she believed his story. He asked her to pray for him, because he thought God would listen to her prayers. Anna assured him that she did believe in what he recounted and wished him a better life. It was apparent that he had changed. He also vowed to undo all that was wrong in his life. For the things he could not change, he sought forgiveness.

Anna never saw him again after this, but she knew that Bill would always believe that God had given him more time in this world to seek redemption for something terribly wrong he had done and to avoid eternal punishment in hell. Lately, Anna had begun to doubt that hell really existed. Neither did she really believe in the doctrine of original sin that taught that all humanity was contaminated by the sin committed by Adam and Eve. Why did God plant that tree of knowledge in the middle of the Garden of Eden when he had known beforehand that they would eat the fruits of good and evil anyway? It did not make any sense to test their free will if God had known the result from the beginning of time. If there had been no tree of knowledge, what would the death of Jesus on the cross account for? As for Bill, why did God give him and not others a second chance?

Unlike her grandfather's experience, Bill came back to life and told Anna everything he had seen and heard, along with all activities around the table where his body lay. That surprised her and led her to believe that Bill's soul or consciousness or something had actually gone out of his body for a short journey before entering back into the body.

Bill thought that God had given him a second chance, while others might explain it by saying that his time had not come yet. Whatever the purpose was for Bill to come back to life must have been determined not by his free will, Anna reasoned, but by some supernatural entity, namely God.

Concerned that Anna was thinking too much about NDEs after Bill's event, her friends told her to forget about it. "After all," they told her, "there have been so many of those happening here, and nobody seems to care." Anna realized that what her friends said was true, because people were always in a rush when working in the medical field. There is little time left over for family, and much less for personal cares and thoughts. In addition, the stigma of this "extraordinary" story could impact her negatively as she began her career.

2

Nevertheless, though very busy with daily tasks, Anna could not discharge NDE from her mind. And a new concern emerged: What is the path of a soul after leaving the physical body? Is it the same or different for everyone? What is the nature of life after death, and what is the journey of a wandering soul?

Unlike other NDE persons, who had contemplated the source of lights from a distance or who had traveled through a tunnel before having their souls pushed back into their bodies, Bill had traveled in the dark and was permitted to return only after being immersed into burning fire. In both circumstances, it seemed to Anna, once having left the body, the souls have no choice but to follow the paths assigned to them, which matched the teaching by most religions. Growing up, Anna had learned to believe that once leaving the physical body, the soul of a person will go either to heaven or hell after immediate judgment. There was no time for a soul to stay behind, making contact with the living. By this reasoning, ghosts or supernatural phenomena could be only figments of the imagination. But seven months into her second year of internship, Anna encountered such a "figment" or "illusion" as characterized by those who didn't believe in such things. But Anna thought of her experience as meeting a "wandering soul" or "a friendly ghost."

Before the changes that regulated the maximum working time for interns, it was known to most of the medical students that the second-year internship was the busiest and hardest for most residents. They were often sleepless for thirty-six to forty-eight hours and under the constant pressure of hard and intense work. Even a few minutes of sleep were very precious. The veterans hospital reserved a small bed in a nine-by-five-foot room on the lowest floor for the on-duty interns to take a quick nap when their work checklist was complete and there were no urgent calls.

On one occasion, sometime after two a.m., after having slept about five minutes, Anna was awakened to pronounce a patient's death, which was one of her duties as an intern. She was called by a nurse to a patient, Mr. Gordon, who had just died and needed to be pronounced. It was a long walk from the nap room to the elevator.

It was January in Kansas City, and snow had been falling incessantly for two days and nights. The whole veterans hospital was quiet and asleep under snow and freezing weather. The hallway seemed deserted, cold, and even longer at this hour of the night. There was no one at the entrance of the elevator, and it took awhile to descend from the top floor. When the elevator finally arrived, it seemed to take longer than usual for the door to open, as if someone was trying to hold it back for some reason. When the door finally opened, a gust of very cold air rushed out in Anna's face, and something like a thin layer of fog blurred her eyes as it blew out from the inside of the elevator. After waving away the mist, Anna saw a man standing inside. He seemed very friendly and smiling.

In a rush to get the work done and go back to her rest, Anna did not pay too much attention to the man nor wonder where he was going at this late hour of the night. She only remembered his happy face and his hands shoved inside the pockets of a black coat. However, she tried to engage him in some small talk. "Good morning, how do you do? It is really late and cold outside...." But only Anna did the talking; the man just smiled and nodded in return.

She was so tired that she did not think of anything else before she got off the elevator. Anna walked out and forgot to say good-bye to the man. Behind her, the elevator closed and ascended to a higher floor. Entering the room where she was called, the nurse on duty gave her all records and papers that she needed to check and sign after examining the cadaver. Before signing the documents, as routine, she and the nurse walked to the place where the body of the dead man lay.

When seeing the face of the deceased, Anna made a loud, surprised sound. The nurse was startled, believing that Anna must have recognized an acquaintance. Anna stared in disbelief at the dead man on the gurney; he had the same smiling face as the man she had just left inside the elevator.

Anna would later learn that Mr. Gordon's record indicated that he had no brothers, twin or otherwise. If he had no close relatives, then who was it in the elevator? Lacking proof of any alternative, she came to believe that the man she had met in the elevator had to be Mr. Gordon, the same man whose death she was going to certify.

3

Anna believed she had met the spirit of a dead man, a ghost. She asked herself if it were likely that she should be able to see ghosts in physical form. Though she had heard many ghost stories, never before had she seen a ghost, nor did she previously believe in ghost stories. But she truly believed that it was Mr. Gordon who had appeared to her inside the elevator. It was real, but she dared not tell anyone at the time, because on the one hand, her position as a doctor and a scientist discouraged her from disclosing "nonsense" stories such as ghosts or apparitions. Furthermore, it was widely accepted that there were no such things as ghosts, which were only the products of imagination or hearsay.

On the other hand, however, Anna knew that contrary to public opinion, quite a few of her colleagues had told her many stories of ghostly appearances, and most of them felt fear when walking into the morgue alone, even in the daytime. Anna was among them. In fact, upon reflection, she found it odd that she had no eerie feeling whatsoever when talking to Mr. Gordon inside the elevator; though silent, he had been very friendly and warm.

For quite a while, Anna was not concerned about ghosts anymore after encountering Mr. Gordon, but she was perplexed by the purpose of his appearance. Why did he want to meet her inside the elevator? Why was he wandering around? Why was he not leaving this suffering world and hurrying to the divine heavenly realm, full of joy and happiness? It seemed he had some reason to meet her and was waiting for her inside the elevator.

Could it be that he had not admitted to himself that he was dead and was wandering around the area, unable to leave until his demise had been confirmed by her? Was he waiting for Anna, rather than the nurses, to witness his departure from this ephemeral world? Perhaps he knew she was coming and sent the thin mist as a signal, to tell her it was he, the dead, waiting to say good-bye to her. Anna thought of the fog, the mingling of cold and hot air, on a very cold night. If it was a signal, she had not gotten it. She hoped that Mr. Gordon would forgive her for this. But could he be permitted to stay around and not depart on the path assigned to him? There could be reasons for him to linger that were beyond her understanding. One good thing coming from meeting with Mr. Gordon, however, was that Anna no longer feared the dark or ghosts. Maybe that was Mr. Gordon's last task to fulfill before going away.

Anna also thought about the appearance of Mr. Gordon's body. How could she have seen him exactly as in his real body? What allowed him or his soul to take any form or shape it chose? From her experience, Anna wondered whether she would believe from now on in the many ghost stories that she had previously ascribed as nonsense or products of overworked, exhausted imaginations.

On the one hand, this first experience with the reappearance of the dead gave Anna confidence and courage to work with dying persons. On the other, it stirred up in her great confusion about the wandering soul. Apart from her own religious teaching, she knew that each culture had different beliefs about the path of the soul following death. Mr. Gordon's appearance to her fit no explanation that she knew of, either from religion or science. As an intern, Anna kept this secret to herself, not wanting to jeopardize her career as a scientist. She hoped that with time and more probing, she could make some discoveries about this mystery.

As time passed, her residency was about to end. Anna came to realize that once in a while, she happened to know about something that was about to happen before it took place, even though she did not know why or how she had known it. Was it extrasensory perception, premonition, or some other sixth sense that came to her mind? At first she did not trust it much, but then she used it to save the life of a patient.

His name was Paul, and he was brought into the ER with stomach pain. A thorough initial evaluation did not reveal any abnormalities. However, he was admitted into the hospital in the afternoon. That early evening, there was no sign of any problem. However, when doing her routine checking, Anna felt very strongly that something bad was going to happen to Paul, though she did not know what. She did not know why she was so sure about it, but before leaving the room, she instructed a first-year intern on duty to sit at Paul's bedside, watch him very carefully, and report to her immediately about any status changes. The other intern asked if Anna could tell him why, but she only told him to do as she requested. Actually, she knew there was no way to explain it to her colleague.

The intern woke Anna up in the middle of the night, reporting an irregular heart rhythm. The patient had complained only of stomach pain when admitted, so Anna had no idea what the connection could be. Still, she decided to do an echocardiogram of his heart.

The procedure revealed blood clots that with each heart pump showered his stomach with clots, preventing blood flow to his stomach and bowels. Paul was sent immediately to surgery and survived. Had it not been for Anna's extrasensory perception, Paul probably would have died and no one would have known why.

Anna did not know how, when, or from where she got ESP. Was it bestowed by God or inherited from parents? It could be both. Anna reasoned that her ESP could have been passed down from her mother, who had once recounted an experience that took place in 1972 in Vietnam. While working at a business shop one afternoon, suddenly Anna's mother felt something strongly disturbing. She tried to calm down, but in vain. The disturbing and burning sensation became stronger and stronger; her head seemed to spin around so that she could not do any work, and she felt some kind of force urging her to go home. Unable to appease the urgent call, and since there was no home phone in Vietnam at the time, she closed the shop and hurried home. On passing through the front door, she saw her son, who, under his grandfather's care, was shaking violently because of high fever and convulsions, and his grandfather had no idea how to deal with it. She grabbed her son and rushed him to the hospital, where the boy was saved.

Later, asked by her parents-in-law how she had known to come home just in time, her answer was that she did not know how she knew.

The correct answer would be that she was alerted by ESP.

In a similar way with Paul, her patient, Anna did not know why something dangerous was going to happen to him. She just knew it. Most would dub such an experience a "sixth sense."

In general, a sixth sense is understood as a form of perception that enables someone to know something ahead of time or from a distance. However, as Dr. Dexter from Saint Mary of the Plains College had pointed out, actually there are more than five or six senses, probably many more than are thought to exist. Feeling the approach of danger is one of them; almost everyone feels danger for himself—even animals do. But not many know or feel danger for others, as Anna did for Paul.

At first, Anna considered ESP a mystery, but after research and consulting with others, she attributed it to some sort of mental waves. According to Anna, each individual has different kinds of waves. Only a few people have this special kind of wave we call ESP.

In the case of Anna's brother, his soul sent out the waves telling the world that he was in danger. Meanwhile, the soul of Anna's mother, having some type of special receiver—perhaps because of the maternal bond—caught the frequencies from her son urging her to come rescue him. In a similar way, Anna's consciousness had received the call from Paul's soul informing her of the urgent situation, leading to her directive to her colleague to report any changes in Paul's status.

From this incident, Anna was very glad to discover that she was also bestowed with this special tool that could help her career immensely. She also learned from it the lesson that a medical doctor could save a life in many different ways. Anna considered the ESP experience and others as gifts from God during the years of internship to enrich her and enable her to better fulfill her task as a physician in the next phase of her career, which was about to begin.

CHAPTER 6
JOURNEYS INTO MYSTERY, LOVE, AND DIVINITY

I

Armed with knowledge and experiences from three years of internship, Anna, along with two other doctors, sought a loan to set up a medical practice in Kansas City, Kansas. It was not very far from the veterans hospital, and the group worked in parallel with the Saint Joseph Medical Center.

The business prospered gradually, but revenues were still far from enough to cover the expenses for a couple of years.

For the first few months of the private practice, the material world and the needs of her practice dominated most of her time, at home and at the office. Anna had been married since the beginning of her residency. Her husband, Mike, whom she married on June 4, 1994, was still in school, pursuing some kind of career that was unknown to her. Her daughter, Emily, was born on August 9,

1999, during her first year in private practice. She had little time with Emily after work. Each working day, she came to the hospital to visit and check on patients for a couple of hours before returning to the office for the incoming patient visits. At the time, most of her patients were old ladies, and Anna felt very close to them. It could be that she saw in them the image of her own lovely grandma.

One of them was Linda Johnson. Mrs. Johnson, a patient with lung cancer and other complications, had her first visit with Anna about one week after her medical office opened, and she chose Anna to replace her primary-care physician, who had just moved out of the state. After about four months, Mrs. Johnson's health situation got worse and she was hospitalized.

To Anna, Mrs. Johnson seemed very lonely. There was no one to call or visit her at all. She confided in Anna once that she had married her high school sweetheart, who, after they had two children together, ran away with another woman. Her daughters, Katie and Laura, had both eloped, leaving home and never calling back. Mrs. Johnson seemed not to blame them for abandoning her and admitted her fault for not taking good care of them; she had begun drinking and smoking heavily after her husband's abandonment.

Anna had directed her to quit both habits, but it seemed too late to save Mrs. Johnson's lungs. Her financial status was fine. Right after her husband and children left, she amassed a big sum of money, inherited from her grandfather. The inheritance had been delayed by litigation with other claimants, and Mrs. Johnson stayed quiet about the money until after her husband and children had left her.

But now, she wished that her daughters would call so that she could be with them. To avoid loneliness, Mrs. Johnson raised birds—a lot of them. Some were rare, beautiful birds she bought from South America, some were from Asia, and some were local species. Some were very big; some were tiny. She also claimed that she could communicate with her birds and that they understood her. She had to pay for a neighbor boy to feed her birds whenever she was away from home or, as now, in the hospital.

When she realized that her house was on Anna's way to and from work, Mrs. Johnson gave Anna keys and asked her stop by occasionally to check on the birds and the house. Though very busy, Anna did as Mrs. Johnson bid. As for Anna, she looked at Mrs. Johnson as her grandmother, treating her with love, compassion, and sympathy. Their visits were like those between members of a close family, not of a doctor and patient. Breathing with difficulty, Mrs. Johnson reminded Anna of her own grandmother's struggles to suck air into her lungs on the last day of her life. Mrs. Johnson felt Anna's compassion and wished that she could do something for her in return. There were strong bonds between them.

One afternoon, on the way home from her office, Anna sensed that something was going to happen that involved Mrs. Johnson. She sensed a need to check things at Mrs. Johnson's house. Everything was fine there, including the birds; there was nothing out of the ordinary. When Anna was about to lock the front door, a taxi drove into the driveway. A young lady and a child, a small girl, got out and walked toward Anna. From the woman's resemblance to Mrs. Johnson's stature, Anna knew this lady must be one of her beloved patient's daughters. After greeting them and identifying herself, Anna asked both mother and child to get into her car and drove to the hospital.

As they conversed on the way, Anna got to know the lady,

who was the younger daughter, Laura. The older one, Katie, had unfortunately died in a drunk-driving accident along with her husband—or boyfriend: Laura wasn't sure which—in El Paso, Texas. Laura claimed that she had called her mother a few times but got no answer. About two months earlier, she related, her husband had left home and never returned. One of his acquaintances told her he had been killed at the border, on the Mexican side. She said that while she was living with him, her husband never wanted her to call her mother, to avoid having his address known. After his death, she sold whatever she could to come up with enough money for the trip for herself and her daughter to Kansas City.

Anna provided Laura with the details of her mother's sickness, telling her that her mother's time left on earth would be only a matter of days. Anna told her that her mother had a great love for her and her sister. She had wished that she could see both of them before she died. Laura listened, and tears flowed incessantly from her remorseful eyes.

Mrs. Johnson was asleep when they came to her room. To avoid an emotional shock, Anna walked in to wake Mrs. Johnson up while Laura and her daughter waited outside the door. Anna asked Mrs. Johnson what she would say if one of her daughters came to see her in this room: Would she be happy or unhappy, angry or moved?

Her answer was she had nothing but love for her daughters. Her voice, though feeble, was audible to Laura at the door. Without waiting for the signal from Anna, Laura rushed through the door and put her arms around her mother's neck and cried. Mrs. Johnson cried, too. They all cried together for some time before Laura remembered to call in her daughter, Lisa, to introduce her to her grandmother.

Mrs. Johnson's situation got worse; her lungs were past all hope. Her pain became unbearable, and Anna prescribed morphine to assuage it. Mrs. Johnson fell into a coma and died four days after her daughter Laura returned. Later, Laura told Anna that before the moment of death, in a very short time of consciousness, her mother said she was grateful to Anna and wished that she could return her kindness in any way possible.

Mrs. Johnson died and was buried like any other patient. Most such patients would be forgotten in no time. But something was special about Mrs. Johnson. It seemed that Anna had a role to play, to bring back love between mother and daughter, to fulfill a patient's wish before she went into the other world.

Five days passed after Mrs. Johnson's funeral, and one afternoon at about six thirty, wrapping up a long working day and preparing to go home, Anna, while closing the windows and looking down at the parking lot of her building, saw a lady dressed in black standing close to her car, waving up at her. The lady resembled Mrs. Johnson, and Anna guessed it was Laura wanting to ask something about her mother. The sky was dark and the air felt as if rain was about to start.

Anna hurried to her car and as she reached it, she realized that the parking lot was vacant; there was no one to be seen. Where was the woman in black? Anna honked her car horn and waited for about three minutes. Still no one appeared. By now, the sky was dark and a light drizzle had begun.

Anna decided that she had seen either an illusion or some sort of reflection from the storm; she left the parking lot and started home. The roads were deserted and wet. Anna accelerated, hoping to reach home before the storm worsened. As Anna approached an intersection at high speed, suddenly a big bird veered out of nowhere, straight toward the front windshield, almost completely blocking Anna's view. She slammed on the brakes, and the bird veered left and escaped an instant before hitting the windshield.

Anna's car slid and stopped in the middle of the intersection, barely avoiding a collision with another car that had run the stop sign. The driver of the other car stopped and ran to Anna to see whether she was hurt. It was a young man about twenty years old, who admitted he didn't see the stop sign. He then asked Anna how she knew he was coming and was able to stop in time. Anna brought herself back from her terrified moment and told him about the bird. The man replied that he saw no bird at all. The man apologized several times for his misdeed and left. The other driver denied seeing it, but Anna was sure a big bird had saved both her and the man from a collision.

For many days afterward, Anna did not know how to explain why the bird had zoomed in and then flown away at just the right moment to avoid the crash. The calculation was more precise than any computer. Anna came to believe that only by a supernatural intervention did she survive. She remembered how Mrs. Johnson had repeated several times that she would return the favors. Anna decided it must have been Mrs. Johnson who stood waiting at the parking lot and who had followed Anna on the journey home. It was certainly not Laura, who later confirmed that she had not gone out of the house on that day.

Anna had no way to know for sure the identity of the lady at the parking lot, but she accepted the fact that it was Mrs. Johnson, the bird lover, who stayed around in this world to fulfill her promise of returning a favor to Anna by transforming into the shape of a bird to stop her car from wrecking. Though this was Anna's strong belief, she knew it was just a supposition and that she would be unable to make other people believe it was Mrs. Johnson who had rescued her.

2

After the accident, Anna was obsessed by birds and ladies in black. Each time she opened or closed the office window, she always looked down at the parking lot to see if anyone was standing there. While driving, she looked around for any bird in sight. Like Mr. Gordon, who appeared to Anna once in the elevator and went his way, probably into the heavenly realm, Mrs. Johnson had appeared only once, to save her from an accident. There were no further signs of her after that. It could be that both Mr. Gordon and Mrs. Johnson were free of all attachments to this bodily world and moving toward the next stage assigned for them. Anna's obsession gradually faded away as she resumed her busy workload with her patients.

Also standing out among her patients was Mrs. Mary Thomas, a wealthy widow who was referred to Anna by friends and chose Anna to take care of her in her last years of life. Her rich husband had died of cancer five years earlier and left her with a huge fortune. Her only son went missing in action during the Vietnam War and had never been heard of since. Once more, Anna had another patient who was connected to the Vietnam War.

Mrs. Thomas suffered from a rare disorder of the lungs. In her last days on earth, she was admitted to the hospital as she struggled to breathe. As Anna came to Mary's room the last morning before she died, she was sitting against a pillow leaning along the wall. She seemed quite energetic, alert, and sober, and requested to talk to

Anna. They had some wonderful, intimate discussions together that morning. During the course of conversation, Anna aimed at bringing Mary calm and peace about her imminent death. Mary said to Anna, "Don't worry, my dear doctor. I have no fear of dying."

She saw that Anna seemed very surprised. Then, to Anna's further astonishment, Mary added, "I am expecting it."

"You are expecting your death?"

"Yes, I know my time on earth is coming to an end, because I was informed ahead of time about many things that are about to happen." Looking at Anna, she asked, "Do you believe me?" Without waiting for an answer, she continued, "I know you do not believe anything of what I just said. However, you know that some people see and hear things that others don't; they could also feel and know things that are going to take place." Mary stopped again. She seemed tired, but then, with a rather clear voice, she continued, "I can see things that others cannot, and I know that you and I have been related in some way previously, in a different space and time than this bodily world; that was the reason I chose you to be my doctor for my last days of life."

Anna worried as she listened to Mary, thinking that her mind had gone awry. When Anna was about to leave, Mary reached for her hand, squeezed it tightly to hold her back, and said, "I have met your son."

"I do not have a son, only one daughter, as I have told you before," Anna answered. "I have never introduced my daughter to you."

"I did meet your son," Mary persisted. "You have not met him, but you will soon."

Perceiving that Anna had not paid any heed to what she was

saying, Mary tried again, speaking louder. "You may think that I am out of my mind. No, I am not. I told you so, because I want to return the favor of all the time and work you have done to take care of me."

A light remorse touched Anna's heart. She did not want to hurt Mary's feelings at the very last moment. She turned, grabbed Mary's hands, and said, "Mary, I believe you and I thank you for your information, but how do you know it was my son? Where was it that you have met him—in your dreams, or in person?"

"I cannot explain how and where I met your son. I met him someplace else, in another world."

"You recognized his face and you knew it was a boy?" Anna asked in a happy voice that made Mary smile.

"Yes, I know his face. It is a boy. No doubt about it."

"How do you know or who told you he would be my son?"

"Nobody told me. I just know it."

Anna still did not pay much attention to what Mary said. She thanked Mary for the information and was about to leave, having lots of work to do. But before Anna left, Mary added, "I am just a messenger. In a short period of time, your son will come."

On the way out, Anna still heard Mary repeating that her son was coming soon. She thanked Anna for her care and wished her the best.

Anna pretended to believe the information to please Mary. She still thought that Mary's mind was not really with her anymore. Further, Anna had no intention of having more children, because her marriage seemed to be going through some difficulties and she feared that it might not last much longer. The relationship between Anna and her husband had turned sour only a few months after their wedding, before the birth of her daughter. She had thought about divorce several times, but dared not bring it up.

For one thing, she hoped the situation would change, and for another, her parents had told her beforehand that she should think twice about her choice of husbands, since there had been no such word as divorce in the family's dictionary.

But because Anna was Vietnamese and her husband was white, there were frequently angry arguments about differences in customs, food, smells, money decisions, and a lot more. After each quarrel, her husband apologized and promised to change. Anna clung to the hope that he would change, though her father had warned her and her fiancé before they were married that there would be no changes in personality or nature of anyone during the course of marriage. Each one must learn to accept the other as he or she is. Where there was no acceptance, there was no happiness, he told them.

Regardless of their many differences and arguments, she and her husband had so far stayed together as a couple for the sake of their child. But Anna had still decided not to have any more children for the time being.

For all these reasons, Anna did not give much weight to what Mrs. Thomas had said, but the story became an anecdote she shared with her friends as they chatted, from time to time.

The medical practice was not going as well as Anna expected. With the huge restrictions from insurance companies, the money collected was not enough to cover monthly expenses. Financial problems and material needs became primary concerns for Anna. Her parents had to intervene to rescue her from bank foreclosure on their house; meanwhile her husband seemed ignorant of what was going on. There was no time to think about spiritual matters or life beyond this world. Her pride as a doctor did not permit Anna to reveal her desperate financial status. She quietly sought a way out.

One Friday night Anna went to bed late, exhausted from considering various plans for her struggling business and laden with worries. She dozed off after midnight and had a dream. In her dream, her grandmother came to her smiling and told her not to worry. She told Anna that going to Texas would be best for her. Waking up in the early morning, Anna's memory of her grandmother's message was still vivid. Why Texas, Anna wondered. Then she reasoned that what she had heard in the dream was less likely to be a message from her grandmother than some form of subconscious wish fulfillment.

Still, an idea came to her when she thought about Texas: Why couldn't she look for employment in other places, including Texas, and give up the private practice? During breakfast, Anna told her husband her thoughts. Mike, her husband, asked her to consider Austin, Texas, where he had some friends who were doctors who might be able to help her. Mike also favored going to Austin for the reason that he had been out of work since they had been married. He had taken several additional courses in college to increase his employability but had been unable to land anything. Unemployed, he had been a heavy burden for Anna during their marriage. Leaving Kansas City could perhaps increase his chances of finding a job. In Austin, electronics, medical, and financial professions were booming. After their discussion, Mike decided to call his friends in Austin first thing on Monday to find out what they might say about a job for Anna.

With the plan agreed to, Anna took off to her office to make a list of what she needed to do and began her inventory of all equipment and supplies to prepare for the closure. As she sat in her chair after more than two hours of checking, counting, and arranging material into categories, the phone rang. It was Mike, calling her to come home immediately. Expecting something important, Anna hurried home, leaving her office in a mess. Approaching the house, she saw an unfamiliar blue car with Texas plates parked in their driveway. Mike opened the door to greet her, then took her to the patio and introduced her to a young man named Jerry Brown, a physician, who Mike claimed was his close friend from high school. Jerry was in Kansas City from Austin to attend a wedding and ran into Mike at the supermarket. Mike asked Jerry if there were openings in Austin for his wife, and Jerry responded that currently there was a huge need for internal-medicine doctors like Anna. Mike thought it would be a good idea to let Jerry stop by for just a few minutes to talk to Anna about everything she needed to know.

Two weeks later, Anna flew to Austin for interviews and was hired as a hospitalist, similar to an emergency doctor, by Saint David's Hospital. Reflecting on all that was taking place, Anna wondered if she were under some kind of mysterious force that was driving her life in a way that was beyond her understanding. She remembered the voice of her grandmother in her dream, telling her to go to Texas. Was it a wish-fulfilling dream or simple coincidence or synchronicity of the meeting between her husband and Dr. Brown? It seemed there was an arrangement for her to be in Austin, Texas, for some purpose beyond her financial situation.

Five months later, settled in Austin and at the busiest time, Anna realized she was pregnant. Though unexpected and previously unwanted, Anna hoped this baby could help to save her marriage. The test confirming her pregnancy immediately brought up her memory of Mrs. Thomas's prediction, though Anna had attributed what she had said as nonsense at the time. Anna avoided having an ultrasound to find out whether it was a boy or girl. During the pregnancy, there were many "what ifs" in Anna's mind: What if it's a girl? What if it's a boy? What if what Mrs. Thomas said was true? What if the belief in reincarnation was also true? What if someone who had known Mrs. Thomas in some other time was born to be her son? She remembered that Dr. Dexter had once said, "Reincarnation is suited well to Christianity for the reason that God could determine which soul would go to the next stage and which one would go back to fulfill something in this bodily world as God sees fit. Besides, where does God get the soul from to assign to a newly conceived body? Of course he does not instantly fabricate it. He must take it from an existing soul coming from whoever just passed away, or one that is on the cosmic 'waiting list.'"

During her pregnancy, whenever Anna was asked whether it was boy or girl, she always answered, "It's a girl." She really hoped that the coming child would be a girl, to prove the folly of all that Mrs. Thomas had told her. In reality, she did not want to accept that there could be truth in Mrs. Thomas's words.

The due date came on March 22, 2004. "I am going to know if it is a boy or a girl," Anna told herself on the way to the hospital.

Being very excited, she did not feel much pain during her labor. And when the infant was delivered, she tried to raise herself up to wait for the obstetrician's announcement. Then she heard, "It is a boy, a fine and healthy boy."

Despite her previous wishes, the news made Anna happy, though she did not know why. She lay down and dozed off peacefully.

Looking at her son's face when she awoke, Anna's mind was bombarded with questions again: Is this the boy Mrs. Thomas had met? Where had they met? How did he look when she met him? How did she know that he would be Anna's son? Mary Thomas had said that she was neither a prophet nor a fortune-teller; she just knew and met Anna's child, and it was a boy who would be Anna's son.

Anna thought about the mystery of conception that went beyond her limit of understanding. At the instant a sperm cell penetrates an egg, a tiny dot is formed and a life seems to begin. From constant division and redivision inside, the dot gets bigger and bigger. Then the heart, the head, the body, and all the parts of a human being come into existence. The same process is true with many species of animals, resulting in different bodies in different species. Anna wondered if her son had met Mary Thomas before his face and body had been designed, sometime before he was born. At that time, his body could have been invisible to most human beings, but visible to some. It even could be that there is no such thing as "invisible." We term it as such because we cannot see it with our eyes, Anna reasoned. Perhaps we view the soul or spirit as invisible because it is made of some unknown, extremely delicate substance that is undetectable by any modern microscope. Perhaps the soul vibrates or emits a wave that only a few are able to perceive. Mrs. Thomas and perhaps certain psychics might be sympathetic to these vibrations in different realms of existence. In fact, Anna realized, to most of us, even now, germs, viruses, bacteria, and many other microbes are still invisible to our naked eyes.

Anna realized that if there were truth in Mrs. Thomas's words, then the heavenly body of Anna's son that Mrs. Thomas had met might be like that of Jesus after his resurrection and that of Mr. Gordon, whom Anna had met inside the elevator of the veterans hospital in Kansas City, Missouri.

Anna also wondered why this soul had chosen her as mother; was it an act of free will, or an obligation? Before coming into being, was there any relationship between her and her son-to-be? Did gender matter to a soul?

Perhaps God had chosen her as a means for her son to come to this world. For human beings and all earthly species, was this the way the very first life had been created? Religion had a simple solution to this question: God made it all and the Bible tells it all. Scientists, however, do not buy what is said in the Bible and try to find the origin of the earth and how life began. They come up with theories such as the influence of interplanetary particles from comets and evolution. But there's no way to prove conclusively whether these theories are true.

Anna thought that even the most intelligent people, who claimed to be scientists and had minds created by God, had limited knowledge of how God worked, certainly in matters that they could not see or touch. Anna tended not to think of herself as a scientist, because she had such incomplete knowledge of medicines, of the body and its internal systems, and even less about evolution and theology. She had, however, been thinking about life after death and about God for a while.

At first, she had many questions about God: What is God? Does he have parents or siblings? If he has no parents, where does he come from? Did he make the big bang or did the big bang make him? What about before the big bang? There are many questions that the smartest scientists, Anna thought, would be unable to answer. As for her, Anna believed there must be some holy, powerful entity that governs the universe. Some people call it God, others call it Creator or Providence, and so on. This identity owned and created everything in the universe. It was a living universe from the very beginning, not a dead one.

Anna had come to believe that God created a universe or universes in which he sowed all kinds of living seeds. In the same way a human body could be created by fertilizing an egg with sperm in a test tube, God had created eggs and sperm of infinite species and spread them all over the universe. He then set up conditions similar to the one in the test tube for eggs and sperm of all species to meet, to react, and develop into beings of each. During the process of formation, each species attracted some special energy or spirit or soul—or nothing, depending on what had been programmed by God for each. Anna reasoned that this thinking was not far from Christian teaching. In the Bible, the process of forming Adam and Eve was not fully explained. With the way of creation Anna envisioned, there might have been several Adams or many Eves rather than one of each. Different Adams and Eves might have lived in different continents on this earth and have spoken different languages. There might be many Adams and Eves on other planets where eggs and sperm found the right conditions to meet and develop. With Anna's theory, there were no more concerns about which was first, chicken or egg. And it was still correct to say that human beings had come from God.

Anna was also curious about other things, such as the personality, nature, and character of a person. Did her son, for example, already carry with him what he would be? Did he inherit his potential from his parents? In Western philosophy, environment is thought to have a greater influence on an individual's personality than heredity, and God has little to do with either of these, even in religious communities and educational systems. Ancient Chinese philosophers, including Confucius, believed that one is born good and virtuous; unfortunately, vice and evil gradually infiltrate one's nature. However, most Easterners' opinions on the character and nature of a person were very clear: "A child's body is born from his parents, while his character and nature are from heaven." The characteristic features may show conspicuously in the face, stature, or general appearance of a person so that he or she can be easily recognized and judged by others about who he or she is. Based on this opinion and her experiences, Anna's grandmother had given advice to her children and grandchildren about how to make better choices for their spouses. Regrettably, Anna ignored this wisdom when choosing her husband.

Anna had to concede, however, that there was some truth in her grandmother's opinion. She could tell if a person was mean or decent, smart or dull, romantic or practical, trustworthy or not by looking at the face. "The face and body tell it all," Anna's grandmother reminded her when she observed Mike. And what she noticed about Anna's husband had turned out to be all too true.

From this belief it followed that Asian people, Anna's parents included, perceive it as very difficult to change persons' natures, because they have been born the way they are. Nevertheless, looking from the East to the West, from ancient to present, and from practices to theories, Anna still had no idea what made up an individual's personality.

There were no answers, of course, for any of her questions, but she was happy because she had a son, no matter that he was foretold. She knew there would not be any scientific explanation or belief about her foretold son. And it could be simple coincidence. However, Mrs. Thomas insisted that she had met him and seemed upset that Anna showed disbelief.

Anna had to admit that she was placing some faith in Mrs. Thomas at that moment. It seemed that there had been a meeting of two souls: one belonging to her son, from somewhere other than the present world, and the other belonging to Mary Thomas. The first was preparing to reincarnate as a healthy boy, and the second was about to leave this world. Anna was coming to believe that she was destined to have a son, whether she liked it or not.

3

Of course Anna loved her son, equally to her daughter. However, for a long period of time when embracing or kissing him, she had a strange thought that she was embracing and kissing an angel, not her son. She named him Johnny, and he was a happy and handsome boy. Johnny took after his father in everything except his shape of face, which looked like Anna's. Whenever looking at Johnny, Anna tried to find something special about the boy, but she found nothing; he was perfectly normal, like any other boy: eating and sleeping, crying when hungry or uncomfortable, smiling and happy when being held. Sometimes, she brushed off what Mrs. Thomas had said, considering it mere coincidence, but other times, she thought there must have been something that induced Mrs. Thomas to say what she did. She had, after all, asked to meet Anna to inform her about her coming son. The image of the boy Mrs. Thomas saw could have been that of the soul that would become her son.

Anna came back to work only five days after delivering Johnny. She loved her job at Saint David's Hospital. However, she belonged to a doctor's group that charged 20 percent of what each member of the group made. Anna saw the unfairness of this and called for a meeting of the doctor members to protest the high fee. When the negotiation failed, the group nominated Anna to deal directly with the hospital administration. The administration agreed to sign a new contract with Anna's group and cancelled the old one with the previous group. Any new member of the group only contributed 5 percent of what he or she made for the first two years and paid nothing after that. The 5 percent charge would be used for the administrative expenses of the group. Having accomplished this, Anna became popular not just among doctors and administrators of Saint David's Hospital, but also with those of all other hospitals in Austin. Outside of the hospital, she had not yet found any acquaintances.

Early one Saturday morning while at the hospital, she was called to the hospital office. On arrival, Anna saw a security officer holding a small package wrapped in some oily papers. The officer told Anna, "I have a problem here and I think you can help." He then showed Anna the box and continued, "This package was found last night in a pocket sealed under the shirt on the left side of a man who seemed to be having a severe heart attack. He was brought into the emergency room by a young man who reported, in broken English, that he had met this man three days ago in front of a bus station. He came here to look for someone he knew. He had no place to stay, and the young man took him home. He drank too much on Friday night and suddenly fell out of his chair onto the floor. The young man rushed him to the hospital. He said he would be back if he found his identification papers. The young man hasn't come back yet. He might never come back and no one really knows where he is. The heart attack victim died, and his body is in the morgue, waiting for family. There was no information or identification about this man. The only thing we found is this package with some writing that seems to be in Vietnamese, so the dead man is Vietnamese, I believe. That's why your help is needed."

The officer laid the package on the table and asked Anna to open it. When she did, she found a small bundle of hair and a very old newspaper clipping. The paper had turned yellow and the writing on it was indeed in Vietnamese. Anna translated it:

URGENT MESSAGE
My very dear wife Lan Huong,
Where are you? When you read this
please forgive me and bring the baby home.
It's not your fault. It was mine.
I cannot live without you. I love you. I will wait for
you and look for you for the rest of my life.
Your husband,
Thanh Phong

Both Anna and the officer knew whose hair it was. The officer felt disappointed, and after thinking awhile, suggested to Anna, "In my opinion, as a popular Vietnamese doctor, you can help by asking around the Vietnamese community to see whether someone may perhaps know some relatives of the dead man."

Anna knew that would not do any good, because she was new in this city and without much contact with the Vietnamese community. However, she did not want to disappoint the officer and told him that she would try, but that he should not have too much hope in her success. He then made a copy of the message and gave it to Anna.

On the way home, Anna stopped by an Asian grocery to buy food and recognized some old acquaintances, My Thu and her son Phu Sinh (or Peter Nguyen, an "Amerasian," as he was called, being half American and half Vietnamese). Peter had gotten his MD from the University of Kansas School of Medicine three years after Anna. But she had gotten to know him when his mother brought him to the city where her parents were living. Ms. Thu, who already spoke fluent English when she arrived in the United States, easily got a job as an interpreter at a government office. She raised her son, Peter, in a very strict way and isolated him from most of his surroundings with disregard to what people said about them. Peter was a very good son, smart and always obedient to his mother. My Thu seemed distant and sad most of the time. She never smiled and avoided the Asian community except for Anna's parents. Vietnamese regarded her as arrogant and hated her, but she seemed not to care at all. Her goal was to save money to pave the way for her son to become a doctor. As Ms. My Thu expected, Peter made it to medical school and became a doctor, and then mother and son moved away from everyone who knew them. On that Saturday, they happened to stop at the grocery and met Anna by chance.

After greeting and exchanging personal information, addresses, and telephone numbers, Anna recounted the circumstance she had just encountered in the hospital, hoping that Ms. Thu or Peter might know or suggest an idea that could help her locate the dead man's family. Ms. Thu seemed disinterested until Anna mentioned the urgent message; then she became more and more intense and emotional as the story went on. Anna did not notice this at the time, but Peter saw the changing mood on his mother's face as Anna continued recounting the content of the message. Tears slowly fell from her eyes and then suddenly, she fell into her son's arms when Anna said the last two words: Thanh Phong.

When they were finally able to walk her outside the shop, My Thu wept incessantly and asked Anna to take her to the hospital. At the hospital, after demanding to see the original message, she identified herself as a family member of the deceased and agreed to be responsible for the expenses of the funeral and burial. The hospital official was very glad and thanked Anna for the job well done. Both Peter and Anna wondered who the man in the morgue was and how he was related to Ms. Thu. Having confidence in Anna, Peter promised to tell her everything when he found out about it.

Peter later told Anna that on the way home that Saturday, his mother was very quiet and tears never ceased running down her face. They did not say a word to each other. She skipped dinner, locking herself in her room. A few minutes before midnight, Peter realized that his mother was still awake and crying while lying on her bed.

He came and kneeled at her bed and said to her, "Mom, you are all I have in this world. I can't stand that you are miserable and I don't understand why. As I got older, I realized that you were hiding many things from me. I think that you have kept many things to yourself, because you did not want to hurt me.

"But I have always sensed there is something. I know every night you cry silently after shutting the door. So many times I would have liked to ask you who my father is and how I can find him. But something has prevented me from doing so, because I knew these questions would hurt you.

"However, tonight is different. I have to ask you to let me know what it was that made our life miserable. Who is the man who, upon hearing only his name, caused you so much pain?"

My Thu cried louder as her son's voice stopped. Peter was waiting for his mother's reply. In about five minutes, though it seemed like hours to him, she arose from the bed without looking at her son, walked to a desk drawer, and pulled out a thick notebook. She brought it back and sat on the bed facing her son, who was still kneeling.

Putting a hand on Peter's head and still in tears, she told him, "I knew from the day you were born that you would one day ask me these questions. Yes, I have a secret, and I hid it from you and others because I had no other choice. I also knew that I would have to tell you everything one day, and it seems that fate has set it for tonight."

She handed the notebook to him, asked Peter to hold it, and said, "Take this book. Read it and you will know everything you want to know. After reading it, you may despise your own mother as you will." She pulled him to his feet and demanded, "Read it and sleep. You will need some rest. I need you tomorrow."

The son returned to his room and read. His mother's past gradually unfolded before his tearful eyes.

Your grandparents named me Lan Huong. I was born and raised in a wealthy, educated family. Being an only child, my parents loved me so much and would do anything that suited me. I was sent to famous schools to ensure a better future. During school, I met a man two classes ahead of me. At first, I only looked at him as a brother who helped me with homework and gave me advice. Over time and with increasing emotional intimacy, we became lovers. I hid this relationship from my parents for fear that they would neither accept my love affair while in school nor this man, whom they had not chosen. But it was a surprise that when I introduced him to them, they recognized him as their close friends' son and were very happy with my choice. We were lovers in heart and promised to get married when the convenient time came.

The convenient time came when my husband graduated from the school of administration and with his connections was assigned a good position in Saigon. My husband's name was Thanh Phong. I loved him and he loved me, and we had solemnly sworn this love for life.

After our marriage, the sources of income on both sides, my husband's and mine, declined because our family properties were deep in the war zone or had been confiscated by the communist regime. The situation got worse, and everything turned upside down when the United States armed forces started landing in Vietnam. US dollars inflated Vietnamese money so badly that my husband's salary was not enough to buy a bag of rice, while the hookers and bar girls could live like queens with what they made from the GIs. At first my husband protested my applying for a job with USAID. Later, he had no choice but to let me work for this organization. My beginning salary was fifteen times more than my husband's. My work with USAID solved my husband's financial problems, but it was going to bring him worry about family harmony. In order to avoid suspicion or jealousy on his part, I took him several times to my workplace and introduced him to everyone. It seemed he was very content with my work environment and had peace of mind. Among my white American coworkers, there was a particular person who was nice and generous to me and to my husband as well. He seemed to like my husband very much. He bought us expensive gifts on every occasion he remembered. He invited both of us to one party after another. He became a friend of my family. Once in a while, he volunteered a ride home when I had no transportation. With time, he earned our trust completely, for never did he show any sign of misconduct or disrespect to me or my husband.

One weekend this coworker planned a party for his birthday while my husband was out of town for his job. This man was so insistent on inviting me that it was hard for me to excuse myself from coming. Accompanied by a girlfriend, I came to a party for the first time without my husband. During the meal, I only drank soda. Suddenly I felt dizzy and nauseated. I ran to the bathroom, and the man followed to the door to see if I needed help. At the door when I came out, he gave me a pill, saying that I may have caught some kind of virus and that the pill would help. He took me to a room to rest and go home when I got better. Then he went back to the party. Not long after swallowing the pill and lying down on the bed, I fell immediately into a deep sleep. I did not know how long I had been sleeping. In the dreamlike state of deep sleep, my husband came home, lay beside me, and performed the act of love between husband and wife. When waking up, I found myself naked and not in my home. Then I knew what had taken place in that room. I cried and spat at my coworker's face when he came in.

I went home and lived in fear of being pregnant by this white man. My husband came home the next day and never knew about my incident. I never talked to or even looked at the face of the white guy again. He seemed to have no remorse for what he had done to me. I hated myself and was terrified whenever my husband embraced me to show his love for me.

My health deteriorated and I lost my appetite. My face became pale and hollow. The doctor's announcement of my pregnancy made my husband crazy with joy. Even in fear, I still had a hope it would be my husband's child.

He counted each day eagerly to see his first child, who arrived one morning, and my husband, on the way to the hospital, stopped at his office for some important matter. It was a boy and the nurse did not let me see him until he was clean and measured. My husband walked in the room with flowers in his hand right at the moment the baby was brought in for us to see him for the first time. Seeing the baby, my husband dropped the flowers to the floor. His eyes opened wide and his face turned purple. Without a word to me or to the baby, he walked out of the room.

I had seen the baby, too; it was not my husband's son, but the son of the white man. Of course the white man had a name, but I do not want my son to know his name.

Right after my husband's departure, regardless of the lingering pain from my labor, I managed to contact some friends for help. I escaped the hospital and brought the baby to the house of a friend before visits from relatives and before my husband's return. I did not want anyone to see the baby.

Three days later, with the help of a close friend, the baby and I flew to a city in central Vietnam.

The baby is you, my son. I named you Sinh. In Vietnamese, it means "living." But in my mind it came from "sin." You are the son of sin, my sin.

At first, I really hated you for coming to life to destroy my happiness and break the heart of the man I loved. Worst of all, you also brought shame for our families. But before long, I realized that it was my fault, not yours. It was my stupidity in trusting others that destroyed everything. I had lost everything. The only thing I had at the moment was you, my son! Then I looked at you and you smiled, and I loved you and I continue to love you more and more.

I did all the paperwork to change my identity. My new name is My Thu, meaning "animosity against Americans," because in my opinion at the time, thousands of Vietnamese families had been broken since the arrival of the US forces. The girl named Lan Huong did not exist in this world anymore. She had died the night she betrayed her beloved husband.

A benevolent rich man hired me to work as a bookkeeper for his business. I brought you with me and we closed ourselves in a comfortable room reserved for me as an office. I kept you away from the public because people were not friendly with half-breed kids like you. For the same reason, I did not send you to school, and as you already know, I taught you everything at home. You were a very good child: obedient and pious. Never did you talk back to me and you always accomplished what I demanded of you. My goal was to raise you and prepare you to be a doctor. In Vietnam, doctors are the most respected. I perceived that if you became a doctor, you would be a dignitary in the community.

My husband sent many messages in several newspapers and magazines. I knew he would accept you as his son and forgive me, because I knew he really loved me. But I could not forgive myself. Bringing you home, I would disgrace his family's reputation. I cut out and kept all of his messages.

The collapse of the South Vietnamese government in 1975 was a catastrophe. I lost my job, because the new regime seized most of my benefactor's properties. I had to work many odd jobs to have enough food for both of us. Worse, the communists had more hatred for you. They called you "a product of the imperialists." Later, the catastrophe for millions of Vietnamese turned out to be an excellent opportunity for us. Thanks to the "Amerasian Program," which aimed to bring all children fathered by American soldiers left behind in Vietnam to America, we were the first ones to apply, and, thank God, we were among the earliest to come to United States.

Once in America, I returned to my initial goal for you. Even in the United States, Asian people still despise the half-breed kids like you. That's why I stayed away from people except for a few. I was determined to send you straight on the path to being a doctor, and sometimes I am tough on you. Only by becoming a doctor would you gain dignity and would people respect and listen to you.

You have become a doctor.

4

Dr. Peter S. Nguyen and his mother came back to Austin Sunday morning and met Anna at the hospital. Peter filled Anna in on what was going on at home and promised to bring the notebook containing his mother's diary later so she could read it. Ms. My Thu identified herself as the dead man's wife. She brought a marriage certificate and its translation from Vietnamese to English. The young man who brought the dead man in also appeared and apologized for not coming sooner due to overtime work required by his supervisor. After Mr. Thanh Phong's body was carried to the funeral home, all of them followed the young man to his house, where he brought out a small old suitcase. There were some clothes, some money, an Oklahoma driver's license, and a small notebook full of phone numbers and addresses. In one section of the suitcase, one stack of papers contained the documents showing that Mr. Thanh Phong had joined the South Vietnamese army. After the fall of South Vietnam, he was imprisoned for more than five years. When released, he was accepted for emigration to the United States through the HO, or Humanitarian Organization Program, and was settled in Oklahoma City. Also inside the notebook was a piece of paper on which some letters were jotted down: "LH in Austin, Texas." When seeing this, Ms. My Thu knew why her husband came to Austin. Someone must have spotted her somewhere in Austin and informed him.

At the funeral home before closing the casket, Ms. My Thu, with Peter at her side, put in it a wisp of her hair, saying, "My love, here is more hair from me, the hair you had loved to caress when we were together. It is a part of my body that will go with you. I ran away because I did not want to hurt you more. I hoped you would despise me and forget me, though I loved you always. I had read all your messages, and that brought me more pain than if you really hated me.

"You had been looking for me all over, from Vietnam to the United States. When you almost found me, you ran away from me. My dear love, you did not find me; I found you. I have responded to your messages and bring the baby with me as you want. In life you never understood why I had betrayed your love, but in death, you see it now. You may be liberated from sorrow. However, I am not and never will be until I meet you again."

After the funeral, Peter stopped by Anna's home and thanked her for her time and effort in helping his mother. He repeated that his mother would never have met Mr. Thanh Phong without her help.

Having promised to tell Anna the identity of the dead man and how his mother was related to him, Peter handed her the notebook and asked her to read it and return the book at a convenient time. When realizing it was his mother's diary, Anna hesitated and handed the book back. Anticipating this, Peter persisted, asking her to keep the book to read.

He patiently explained to her, "Please feel free to read it. The whole deal is so complicated that I cannot relate to you in words what the story was about. Only by reading it will you be able to know everything. Do not feel bad reading another person's diary. It will be the same if I try to tell you the whole thing. Besides, you and your parents have known us for so long without knowing who we really are. You will do well by reading this. Please read it to share with my mother both the sorrow and happiness of the woman who found her love again and to share with me the feeling of a son who was born without a father."

Peter left and Anna began reading the diary. Anna was stunned when the two words, Lan Huong, appeared. She forgot that this name had been given to her.

The vivid image of the old lady in the hospital in Vietnam came to her mind. She had asked Anna to look for her daughter—named Lan Huong. At that moment, Anna had seen nothing important about looking for a missing daughter, and she had listened to that lady halfheartedly. She had promised only in order to please a sick patient whose mind might have gone wild, and then she completely forgot about it. She realized she should have recognized this name when translating the urgent message.

"It is she, Lan Huong, the missing daughter of the old lady that I met in the hospital in Vietnam, no doubt about it. I have forgotten to seek her, but I have found her anyway, by the will of fate."

Anna called Peter and asked to have a meeting with him as soon as possible. She tried not to talk to Lan Huong for fear of stirring up too much emotion for her at this moment. Sensing something important to his mother, Peter drove to Anna's house at once. Anxiously and urgently, he asked her right at the door, "What is so important and urgent that makes you call me?"

"I have met your grandmother," Anna told him.

Peter stared at her without blinking for a long time in silence. There was a struggle on his face between happiness and sorrow at the news: happiness because he had found his grandparents, but sorrow for the reality that he might be only shame and disgrace for them.

Once inside the house, Anna then related how she had met his grandmother in the hospital and how much that lady had missed his mother and wished to see Lan Huong before her death. Anna asked Peter to tell this news to his mother at the most convenient moment so as not to shock her too much, and she urged that he and his mother should go see his grandmother before it was too late.

"I don't think I should go. Neither would my mother," Peter responded.

"I suggest both of you should go," Anna encouraged him, "for the following reasons. First of all, this is the only chance for you to know your grandparents, whom you have wished to meet for a long time. Both of you should go as soon as you can, for fear that they will not be there for you later. Second, this could be the last wish of an old and sick mother to reunite with a lost daughter and a new grandson."

"But they will look at me as a disgrace for the family," Peter protested.

Anna replied, "Over time, everything has changed in Vietnam. There is no such thing as disgrace or dishonor or morals in Vietnam anymore. Not many care about family reputation or shame as before. As for people like you, it would be an honor for them to have a half-white and rich doctor as a family member."

Looking straight at Peter, Anna continued, "Before, they called you the product of the imperialists. Now, you are the source of finance. Before, they despised you. Now, they highly respect you.

"In all, you and I, we are the children of the war, the Vietnam War. In this war, there were thousands of half-breed children like you. Some unlucky ones were left behind, dragging along in a miserable life. You are among the lucky ones who were brought to the US to have a better life and become a doctor." Anna also told Peter about the African Vietnamese she met in Vietnam who earned a living by selling lottery tickets at restaurants or along the roadsides, shining shoes, or selling fruits and other foods at markets. There were dirty, torn, wounded people, soldiers of the South Vietnamese government before 1975, who wandered along the street as peddlers or begged for food along the streets. They were also the children of the war. And many others were born during it or fought in the war and survived.

Sitting alone in a chair in front of the house as she watched Peter's car speeding away, Anna had a thought that while the Vietnam War had literally ended for most Americans and Vietnamese in April of 1975, it may not have ended yet for Ms. My Thu. She had fought against her will to meet her husband for a very long time. She turned out to be the loser when she found his dead body. And now in her heart another war was to come: the decision whether to bring Peter to meet her parents. For Peter's mother, and for many other Vietnamese and American families with MIA sons or daughters, the war would never end until the missing children were found.

For Peter, the war might never have ended until he found his father. He had vowed to stay single until the day his father was found. However, after reading his mother's story, he determined not to seek his father anymore. To him, his biological father had been the tool sent by the war to destroy his mother's happiness and marriage and to bring him into a disgraceful and miserable life. However, it was also the war that brought him to the United States to become a physician.

As for Mr. Thanh Phong, only at the end of his journey in this world, with the return of his wife, did the war end and he rest in real peace.

Besides the war, true love had played an important role in the dramatic story of Ms. My Thu. Though brokenhearted and betrayed, the man had kept his love for his wife intact; the woman sought to maintain her love by departing from the lover and only returned to unite with him after his death. This could also be a function of different cultures, times, and places. But the true love between Ms. My Thu and Mr. Thanh Phong brought an end to Anna's previous perception that there was no true love between men and women in this world.

5

For a long time, Anna marveled at her involvement in the dramatic reunion of Mr. Thanh Phong and Ms. My Thu. Again, there were many what ifs and wonders: What if her parents had not known Ms. My Thu? What if Anna had not come to Austin, Texas, and had not been in the hospital on that fateful morning? What if she had decided to go home instead of stopping by the Asian grocery store? And was it a synchronicity or a mere accident that she met Ms. My Thu and her son there?

Anna could not believe that everything had happened just by chance; it seemed predestined to take place. Was it true that each individual had a life graph drawn by a supernatural power, or God, along which major events would occur at specific times indicated by the points on the graph? No matter how hard he tried, Anna thought, a man could only change a tiny part of it; the general shape of the graph stayed the same. How did this affect sickness and diseases that cause suffering and death? Were they given to some individuals intentionally from above as opportunities for physicians like Anna to fulfill their life tasks?

However, healing was not the work of physicians only. Anna had heard, read, and watched on television about the work of ministers of different beliefs, and laymen as well, performing healing or talking about miracles of healing coming from prayers. When researching the power of healing or other powers, to evaluate them as treatment for patients, Anna was amazed to learn that there were many divine ways of treatment—more than she could imagine. She was introduced to one of them in Sarasota, Florida, by an adopted brother, H. Van. Since their arrival in America, Anna's parents had established a family tradition for their children to meet together each year in family reunions at different locations during the Christmas season. The chosen place for 2005 was Sarasota, Florida, where H. Van, Anna's adopted brother, was living.

Anna's parents adopted H. Van, a fine boy, at seventeen years old in 1986 when he had just come to the United States from a refugee camp in Hong Kong. He was born during the Vietnam War and it had played a long and especially tragic and dramatic role in his life.

In Vietnam, H. Van belonged to a poor family in a faraway coastal village in central Vietnam where all men, including his father, earned a living by fishing. The village was often caught in the crossfire between South Vietnamese soldiers and communist units. From infancy, H. Van lived constantly with danger and fear. Then one night in 1973, the communists encroached and a fight took place. Several people, including his mother, were killed in the crossfire during the night. He was then four years old. A few months after his mother's death, his father remarried and spent most of his time at sea, leaving H. Van and his younger brother under the care of the stepmother. The life of H. Van turned into hell the day his stepmother walked in and brought with her two sons of her own. She did not allow H. Van to go to school, but kept him home to do hard work. She hit him and deprived him of food for a day or two at a time. Worse, his father came home drunk and was induced by his wife to beat his son even harder.

At fifteen years old, in a secret pact with eight more boys in the village, H. Van planned a daring escape in a very old, small boat given to them by a kind fisherman. One dark night, all nine boys gathered and set off from the beach, aiming for Hong Kong. After more than three days they ran out of food, but kept on. After another day, as their boat came along the coast during the night, they ran out of fuel as well.

At first, they dared not go ashore, because they thought they were somewhere in North Vietnam. They tied the boat to a rock and huddled together in some underbrush, waiting for the morning.

The coming of the morning only brought more fear of arrest. After some thought, two of the stronger boys walked out from the bush and headed to the village. As they drew closer, they saw a Chinese flag. They returned and informed the group that they were in China and were no longer in Vietnam.

Though still afraid that the Chinese might arrest them and return them to the Vietnamese authorities, the boys had no choice but to go to the Chinese village for help; it was either that or stay at the boat to die of hunger.

The boys were very lucky to meet decent people in the village. Though they did not speak the same language, they did their best with their hands to communicate with the villagers, who let them work in the fields for three days to earn enough money to buy enough food and fuel to reach Hong Kong in two more days.

In Hong Kong, all the boys were admitted into a refugee camp immediately and placed as orphans. H. Van went to his first school at this camp, where he learned his first letters in the alphabet with a Catholic monk in a tent school inside the refugee camp in Hong Kong. After fourteen months in the camp, he had learned how to read and write Vietnamese and very little English, along with some basic arithmetic.

He came to Garden City, Kansas, and Anna's parents adopted him, sent him to school, and helped him any way they could. He put his greatest effort into learning English in order to catch up with his classes. He graduated from high school and after two years in college, he earned an associate's degree at the local community college.

H. Van married and settled down in Sarasota. He was assigned as the host of the Vu family reunion for the year 2005. During Anna's stay in Sarasota, H. Van suggested that she should meet a man, named Mr. Cao, who, he said, possessed some kind of divine healing power. When Anna asked what he meant by "divine healing," H. Van answered that he could not explain it. Only by meeting the man would Anna know the whole thing. Pushed by curiosity and inspired by the idea of divine healing, Anna was determined to see the man. The time for the appointment came; there were three participants: H. Van, Anna, and her mother, Mrs. Vu, who wanted to have the healing man tell her about her health.

H. Van had befriended Mr. Cao, a married man with two children, just a few months before. They met at an ice cream store on a very warm afternoon. They had talked, exchanged phone numbers, and become close friends. H. Van discovered Mr. Cao's healing power one day during conversation, when Mr. Cao asked H. Van if everything was fine. H. Van lamented that his wife was experiencing a very hurtful cramp that seemed to endure the entire length of each of her menstrual periods. Her doctor had told them that about one in a thousand women suffered this symptom, and there was no cure.

Mr. Cao volunteered to help. After three sessions of treatment using healing energy, H. Van's wife was completely cured of her pain.

On the day Anna met him, Mr. Cao was waiting for them at the door, and surprisingly, he greeted each person by the correct name; H. Van never gave Mr. Cao any information about Anna or her mother. The introductions were brief, but very cordial and warm. As a close friend of H. Van, Mr. Cao looked at Mrs. Vu as a mother and at Anna as sister. H. Van announced Mrs. Vu's intention and Mr. Cao began his preparation for the treatment. He lit incense and solemnly put it into a small vase on an altar on which sat a Buddha statue and a frame of images of different holy figures. He turned from the altar and asked Mrs. Vu to sit facing the altar.

He instructed Mrs. Vu, "Please, be aware that in the holy world, there is no difference between beliefs. There is only one God. We are going to begin the treatment all the time with prayers. Because I come from a Buddhist family, I pray in the Buddhist ritual. For your part, just sit and relax and do the usual prayers according to your religion's teaching. I know you are a Catholic, so please, pray and ask the Lord Jesus and the Holy Virgin Mary, Mother of God, to be with you to help heal you during the process. In praying, you do not need to tell what kind of illness or illnesses you have. Those to whom you pray will know. If you have some illnesses, it will be the Divinity who cures you, not I, who stands as an intermediary person. Now we start."

Mr. Cao took a seat a foot behind Mrs. Vu. He kept his eyes

closed while his two hands performed movements like those of a dancer behind Mrs. Vu's back without touching her. The speed of the movements changed according to the flow of the energy. After about thirty minutes, he stopped for a fifteen-minute break and then continued the second phase for another thirty minutes.

He would later tell Anna that this was a typical procedure in his way of treatment. Usually he was very exhausted after a session of treatment, but not this time.

He explained that in the first fifteen or so minutes, he tried to gain transcendent energy from his master in the heavenly realm and transfer it to the patient. In the second phase, his energy, combined with that already transferred, would complete the healing. If the energy attracted from Mr. Cao and his master was not enough, the treatment would not occur or not achieve a good result.

Mrs. Vu gained an amount of energy during the first phase. But in the second phase, no treatment occurred, for two reasons. First, Mrs. Vu needed no treatment. Second, Mrs. Vu's master was more powerful than Mr. Cao's. He needed her master's permission in order to go into the treatment.

Anna found this all very interesting. The healing, if obtained, would be thought of as a miracle or the result of holiness, but it was nothing but the work of the mixed energy of two worlds: bodily and heavenly.

The healing process actually seemed very scientific and practical. It seemed a better approach to the cure for an illness than just praying. Anna asked for more information about Mr. Cao's beliefs and teaching.

"This belief has been in the world for thousands of years," he told her. "It is called Mat Tong or Mysterious Original Divinity—MOD. MOD is not a religion. It stands between religion and the science of unknowns. It is a faith that connects the souls of two worlds, the mundane and the holy. Its teaching is based on two very basic principals:

1. One God for all religions

2. One master for each person

MOD, he explained to Anna, maintains that there is only one religion or one God who is the source of power that rules the universe. While living in this world, each person is assigned a master, similar to a guardian angel. The main difference is that a guardian angel is an identity from the heavenly realm assigned to each person by the Divinity, while the master of MOD could be appointed from any world. This master looks after the human to which it is appointed, always to the death. If connected in some circumstances, the master can help the human with healing power for certain illnesses.

"Not every MOD member can access the healing power," Mr. Cao said, "only the righteous who are free from any mischief, whether in actions or in thoughts. And those who can may take many months to learn the healing process. During the process, the patient need not speak out his problems, since the master already knows. The treatment may work well on one but not on another, and the healing process could be longer in one person and shorter for another, just as a medicine prescribed by a doctor may work differently in different persons."

The master chosen by the Divinity could be someone who had

lived in this world several thousand years ago, he said. In Mr. Cao's circumstance, his master had been in this world more than two thousand years before Jesus Christ. Since Mr. Cao was Vietnamese, his master chose his name in Vietnamese. In fact, he lived in a remote country of the Middle East in the long-lost past. When Mr. Cao asked about Jesus, his master simply asserted that he was a powerful man, and nothing else was revealed.

"Jesus, Buddha, Mohammed, Lao-tse, and others are the heralds or sons of God who were incarnated into human form to teach God's love," Mr. Cao said. "They came at different times and spaces to different people, but the love is universal and eternal. Unfortunately, by prejudice, discrimination, stereotype, fanatic beliefs, and all in the name of God, human beings segregate themselves into different denominations to hate and sometimes kill one another."

MOD was like Buddhism, he said, which does not try to convert anybody. The master is not a saint, as in Christianity, whom any follower can ask for help through prayers. Instead, the master is concerned with the spiritual well-being for one individual of this world. If that individual is in need of him or has a desire of healing someone, the master would come immediately when summoned. Telepathy was the way of communication between the master and the individual. Questions and answers are very short, but clear. Doing good deeds, helping people in any way needed, and especially providing cures for sickness were the highest value of an individual in this world. Each individual of this world had freedom to act on his own and accept the consequences of all his actions. The master stands on the sideline not intervening in earthly life unless requested, he explained.

"This terrestrial world is a school where each one must come at least once to learn and perfect himself in order to advance into higher levels closer to God," Mr. Cao said. "Those who do not fare well may have to come back several times. Those who commit misdeeds, instead of advancing, would be sunk into darkness far away from the blissful light of God. No matter what life or universe, each one is still consigned by a master. In order to contact one's master, one needs a referral from another person's master." Mr. Cao made the first connection with his master through one of his older brother's friends, who was an ophthalmologist in Houston, he told Anna. Having known his master only one year, Mr. Cao had saved the life of a young lady with an infected tumor in her head.

The MOD healers never charge patients money, no matter how long it takes to heal. Despite their beautiful achievements, healers like Mr. Cao kept a low profile and stayed humble. They limit their treatments to acquaintances or friends. Not that they are ignorant of people's sufferings; Mr. Cao said that his master once told him that suffering was sometimes a gift from God for those who need it in order to improve and refine themselves.

The next day, Mr. Cao was invited to the family party at H. Van's house. During the tea conversation, H. Van suggested a furnished-energy session for Anna, because she looked very tired. H. Van also wanted to hear from her later about her opinion of the session after she experienced it.

Anna did not say any prayer. She just concentrated her mind, thinking about God and wondering if she also had a master. Mr. Cao stopped the process after about ten minutes. He took Anna away from the earshot of the others and told her, "Yes, you have a master;

my master told me so. There will be upheavals in your life. That is all I was told."

Anna did feel better after the session and was carefree about whatever upheavals might lie ahead. She thought she had been brought into a life full of them.

6

Back in Austin from Florida, Anna found the house empty. Her husband had not yet come back from Kansas, and he left no message on the answering machine. They had had a sort of minor argument about his not going to the family reunion with her and the children. He was determined to go see his half sister in Kansas instead, and he was probably looking for job there. His mood seemed different lately: he was grumpy, complaining of everything. She hoped that he would be better when he got a job.

The house was peaceful without her husband. The children ate and went upstairs; they seemed tired after the trip back home. Outside, it was drizzling and windy. Anna lay on the couch, facing the crucifix hanging above the door. Reflecting on what she had seen and heard in Florida led her into a flow of different, conflicting thoughts.

First of all, was a physician a scientist? Doctors considered themselves scientists; they had learned biology, chemistry, and anatomy, and they memorized all kinds of findings from different research, learned about diseases and their symptoms, and knew medications for their treatments. They then learned how to deal with patients and how to run the business of health care.

Beyond that, Anna found herself not knowing much. She was involved in the science of experiment, not of discovery. Maybe she wasn't a scientist at all. Most scientists deny the existence of ghosts, spirits, supernatural power, or healing power. The reason for their denial could be to avoid a bad reputation or to maintain a good current position. Anna believed in life after death, and wherever there was life, there were activities. These activities or epiphanies could be seen by some, but perhaps not by others.

Her next thought was that there was definitely life beyond death. What that life would be like depended on the teaching of each belief to which people belong. There was no proof of any kind, just faith. And faith came from the Bible, the Koran, the Tibetan Book of the Dead, and so on. The MOD that she had learned about in Florida had neither a book to guide its members nor the demands of a faith. It just revealed a tiny portion of the world beyond.

Next Anna considered that many people believed in guardian angels. Many books told of masters of other worlds and their connections with individuals here, but it was only through faith or in hypnosis that the connection was manifested. However, in MOD, there was direct communication, though in a telepathic mode, between the master and the connected soul of the human being. There was no mention of the souls of other species, Anna noted, having often wondered if that was how we knew animals had no souls. While there was no proof as to whether they did or didn't, humans tended to accept that they didn't, perhaps so that we could kill them for food without guilt. Of course, people killed each other, too, even though they were aware of the existence of souls in other humans.

Anna then turned her line of thought to her struggle with the question of why she had been born into this world. She did not accept that she was merely on the earth to give and receive love, as religions and philosophers might say, or to prepare her soul for eternity. Eighty years or even a hundred years of life had no significance in comparison with the endless existence of eternity, she reasoned, so what could she really do here, in this world, to adequately prepare for going into the unknown realm or the life beyond? Would the life beyond be far better than this one?

This question brought up her memory of her encounter some years ago with a Buddhist monk, a friend of her father. The talk involved many subjects: reincarnation, heaven, hell, life after death, the purpose of life, why one clings to this life and fears to die, and others. The monk stated his idea that each belief has its own way of answering these questions. He took a piece of paper and drew two lines to divide the paper into three equal parts. The leftmost part he marked as "Previous," the middle one as "Now," and the right as "Afterlife."

He told Anna, "This piece of paper stands for infinite times, spaces, or worlds, and two lines separate three different phases of your soul-life—if you believe in the soul. Three words—Previous, Now, and Afterlife—represent three phases of your life."

He showed her the paper.

Previous	*Now*	*Afterlife*

"This is about the circumstances and nature of life," he told her, "not about reincarnation or some other concept you may think of."

He then asked Anna to imagine that she was currently living in the Previous phase. She might perceive herself as a person in a body, as a soul, or just as consciousness. He asked her to imagine further that she was coming closer to the line between Previous and Now, which she would pass over. He added that there were two circumstances for passing over the line: free choice and God's will. If she chose from free will to pass over the line, she must know the purpose of her expedition. If it was God's will, she might not know why God sent her over until much later in the Now. Each language called the act of passing over by a different name, and it is "birth" in English. Each passing over must include the aim of doing something, rather than being for no reason at all.

The monk asked Anna, "If you knew ahead of time all the course of your life in Now, when you were at the line, would you be willing to pass over?"

The question caught Anna off guard. Thinking quickly, she judged that her life had not been very bad so far, but she was unable to say yes or no right away.

Seeing her hesitation, the monk proceeded, "You have a job in Now, whether you came by free will or from God's will. There are very fun jobs, difficult jobs, and interesting jobs, and each individual will get one and get it done in the time between Now and Afterlife. Each job could be only one among several parts of your purpose here on earth. Before passing over, you were equipped with skills for your task. Each person has skills for his own job or jobs. You must fulfill your task, no matter what belief you belong to.

"Now, it is not my intention to wish you there, but let's suppose that you are at the second line, between Now and Afterlife. Would you be very scared?"

Already knowing the answer from Anna, the monk continued,

"Realize that this is not a new line, but the same one that moves from Previous to Now, and the passing over is going to repeat again. Passing over in this sense is called by another English word, 'death.'" It is this word, "death," that causes fear in most people. In reality, it is only a passing over. From this process repeating and repeating, passing over earns another name: reincarnation.

"It is not passing away, either, because the word 'away' has the meaning of 'nowhere.' To say 'you pass away' is the same as 'you are lost' or 'disappeared.' No one knows where you are. Loss or to be missing also brings fear."

The monk told Anna that a soul comes to the line between Now and Afterlife. When past the line, the soul can see something on the other side of the line, but then is pulled back suddenly to the body by a force resulting from some attachment or unfulfilled tasks. If the conditions are right, the soul comes back to the body at once and the life continues. Otherwise, the soul has to wait outside somewhere for the right moment. This is a near-death experience (NDE). What a soul sees on the other side of the line is actually the projection of consciousness of the past rather than the real holy realm.

"Thus, you have no fear if you know that you are going to pass a line as you have done before. You are leaving Now to come to Afterlife, exactly the way you are leaving Kansas to come to Oklahoma at the state line in driving on Interstate 35 South."

Remembering her talk with the monk, Anna could see that his point of view had great value. But she also recognized that Buddhism had influenced his convictions. However, she had to concede that the monk did not mention anything about preparation for the life beyond as most major religions do.

Such preparation was different for each individual in this world, Anna thought. Her life purpose must be something that she was still trying to discover in order to accomplish it.

Anna also thought about the beliefs of the MOD adherents she met in Florida. According to MOD, the earth owns everything that other realms lack, such as bad versus good, suffering and gratification, hatred and love, war and peace, dishonesty and sincerity, and so on. One must pass through the door of this world, a place of schooling, to learn to improve oneself to advance closer to God. If the learning process does not go well, double or triple processes may be needed.

This led Anna to her next line of thinking. When questioned about life in heaven, most would describe a blissful eternity that disregarded those suffering in hell, even family members. But MOD never mentioned heaven or hell. Mr. Cao's master had passed away more than four thousand years ago. Through his work and characteristics, one might think of him as a saint or an angel who lives in a different world not very different from this one. Being in another realm, he becomes ubiquitous like God, and for him there is no limit of time and space.

Anna's final thought focused on the idea that human beings were created by God as "clay in the hands of the Heavenly Potter." Thus, we might all be considered as God's robots. If we are, then the creator could destroy all the robots if their software—their souls—went wrong or became dangerous. If souls came from nothingness, then they could return back to it. All religions' teachings maintained that souls would go into eternity and never perish. But Anna considered that our knowledge is very limited. Even in the future, she doubted that human scientists could discover all God's mysteries, because though robots are sometimes smarter than many, they may not surpass the one who created them.

It could be that "invention" was the wrong term to apply to human discovery. Scientists only try to uncover what is hidden in this universe. And there would be billions of things that were unknown to science. One of them was life after death: scientists generally discount it because they usually perceive any story related to another world as nonsense, fabricated, or, worst of all, unscientific. However, more and more physicians had begun writing about life after death and about contact with the deceased—more than even the psychics. Perhaps this was because doctors hear the last words that patients confide in them before going to another world. For Anna, believing in a better life after death reduced the impact of suffering and brought joy and peace for a dying person, whether he was a scientist or not.

7

Anna went back to work the next morning. The whole hospital seemed different after only one week of absence. The hall looked longer, cold, and deserted. It was the holiday season, and many patients were gone; some had recovered, and some had passed away. There were not many people in the waiting room, either. Anna thought this would be an easy day for doctors.

After diagnosing some patients and having not much to do, Anna walked to her office to check on her past patients' files. Only about ten minutes later, her name was called.

A handsome man, James McDavid, was brought in from his workplace, complaining of severe chest pain. MRI scanning later showed cancer in his lungs and liver. This type of cancer spread very fast and was the cause of his pain.

This news terrified Mr. McDavid. He cried and implored Anna to do anything possible in her power to save him. There were so many reasons he clinged to life: He had a beautiful wife, a two-year-old daughter, and a bright future as chief financial officer of a prestigious company. He earned more than $200,000 per year and lived in a large, luxurious house in Austin. Mr. McDavid had been a successful man and expected a very long and happy life. He felt some light chest pain that came and went, and he had blamed it on long working hours at his office. He had insurance but had never bothered to see a doctor. He considered himself as too young, at the age of thirty-five, to need a checkup.

But cancer had metastasized all over his chest, and now no one could save him. He did not want to die; death had never entered his plans. He had no feelings of sorrow for the deaths of others from accidents, fire, air crashes, or illnesses; these were always somebody else's death, not his or his beloved ones.

Knowing that he had only a week or two to live brought him even greater horror. He wondered why he had to die too young, while others had a beautiful, long life. He feared losing everything that he had worked so hard for. Who would support his wife and daughter?

The more questions Mr. McDavid asked, the more devastation overwhelmed him. He was also frightened because of his lack of a spiritual life. He had been too busy amassing properties and enhancing his reputation to secure his position in this world; he had never thought of his soul. He wondered if he even had a soul, and if he did, where would it go? To hell or heaven? Or to some unknown place?

Great fear overwhelmed him. Never before had he contemplated life after death or reckoned upon God. It was not that he did not believe in God, but he had been too busy with the material world.

Anna tried to calm him down and convince him that he had beautifully fulfilled the duties that God had assigned to him. He had brought love and happiness to his wife and daughter, and prosperity and growth to his business. His life purpose had been attained, and it would be time for him to go to do something else. She told him that perhaps sufferings were a part of God's will for human beings to learn to improve themselves. Anna told Mr. McDavid that his life, though relatively short in comparison with some others, had been full of accomplishment and that his death must have a reason, even though it is not known by human beings.

Gradually, Mr. McDavid accepted his mortal fate without sorrow and fear. At the last moment of his consciousness, he asked God to have pity on him by protecting his wife and daughter. Mr. McDavid died six days later.

Even after having admonished herself several times not to bring patients or their death home with her, Anna still dragged to her bedroom that night two images from the hospital. The first was the countenance of Jennifer, Mr. McDavid's wife. She was stupefied, pale, frightened, and worried when hearing the news of her husband's death. Her body was frozen and her face twisted, her eyes wide open and blank. The second image belonged to Mr. McDavid. Reflecting back to the moment of his death, it seemed to Anna that he suddenly made one last effort to tell her something by looking straight at her while his lips trembled, but failed to make a sound. Anna went to bed and consoled herself. "It could be that he had nothing to tell me."

Anna had a good sleep and woke up about five in the morning. She lay in bed trying to remember all the details of her dream. Mr. McDavid came in the dream, saying that he was fine and asking Anna to pass word to his wife that he loved her and his daughter very much and that he would be with them always. Mr. McDavid looked much younger than before and wore a dazzling white outfit. He was constantly smiling. Immediately Anna thought of her dream as the work of her imagination in responding to her uncertainty about whether Mr. McDavid had something important to say to her. However, her dream also made sense in that Mr. McDavid's wife was not with him at the moment of his death, and he would certainly have wanted her to know that he still loved her from the other world.

Anna knew that everyone had dreams and that she had many nonsense dreams. However, some dreams did warn her of coming events. Anna's memory returned to a dream six years earlier about the son of her adopted brother, H. Van. During the dream, she held a boy in her arms and claimed him as her son. Then she heard a voice from somewhere above her saying it was not hers, but H. Van's. The next day H. Van called and informed her that his wife was pregnant, and she later gave birth to a son.

This circumstance could be coincidence; after all, she had a fifty-fifty chance of being right about the gender of H. Van's son. But another case could not be explained by a lucky guess.

Michelle was Anna's close friend when they were in classes together at the University of Kansas. They often met together during and after graduation. Anna lost contact with Michelle after her move to Austin. One night after five years of disconnection without phone numbers or other contact, Anna dreamed that Michelle called her and told her she was in Austin. In the morning, Anna did not believe in her dream that Michelle was in Austin at all, but she realized she missed her friend and wanted to have information about her. Anna then dug into a notebook in which she had some email addresses more than six years old. She sent Michelle a message, asking her whether she was in Austin. She had little hope that Michelle would receive it. But only thirty minutes later, Michelle called and confirmed she was living in Austin. When Michelle asked Anna how she knew, Anna responded that her dream told her.

Anna strongly believed that humans had souls. In her view, each soul, like a string in a musical instrument, emits different waves during life in this world, and those waves continue in other worlds. Some special souls are able to receive the signals emitted from these kinds of waves. Science may never discover these waves, because souls are invisible and no one knows where the waves come from.

Though believing in some dreams, Anna did not give much weight to the one about Mr. McDavid and decided not to tell his wife, Jennifer, the message. But then there was another important message from Mr. McDavid only three nights later. With the same smiling face and dazzling white clothes, he came in Anna's dream again, asking her to tell his wife two things: "One, stop crying. If you are crying, then there is no time for our daughter. Two, take good care of our daughter."

Anna was not sure whether Jennifer would believe in what she was going to tell her, because there was nothing important or special other than staying away from grief and taking care of the child. But she called Jennifer anyway, hoping for the satisfaction of the departed.

Anna's call had the reverse effect that the dream indicated. The call only reminded Jennifer that her husband was dead and that she was alone in this world to look after her daughter. She cried even harder as she wondered where the money to pay for housing and living for both mother and daughter would come from.

After Anna delivered the message, she considered her business with Mr. McDavid's family done and felt content about it. But she did not know that her psychic channel with the departed was still in use. Less than thirty-five hours after her call to Jennifer, another message came from Mr. McDavid, and it came in a hurry. One evening after dinner while in her study, looking at the mail, checking on bills, and writing letters, Anna had an uneasy feeling that someone was in the room watching her all the time. Though not quite sure of her own sense, she did not want to stay there anymore. She looked at the clock and it showed just ten fifteen. It was not very late, but Anna felt tired and sleepy. She turned off the lights and walked out. Her children were already asleep and the whole house was in a deadly hush. She checked on the children, then went to her bedroom.

She lay down, and sleep came quickly. Mr. McDavid appeared instantly, just as she dozed off. His face was not happy, but also not angry. He thanked her for delivering the last message and requested another one.

"One: do not cry anymore. Take good care of our daughter. Two: do not worry about money. Everything is taken care of and is in a blue folder. Three: everlasting love will be with you both."

Anna woke up at the last word and had no time to ask him anything. Lying in bed, Anna remembered the eerie sensation of being watched that she had in the study. She knew now it was him, Mr.

McDavid, who had been there waiting patiently for her and who had followed her into her bedroom. It seemed he could not come to her in person or talk to her during a waking state; only in sleep could he communicate through her dreams.

Anna also noticed that all his messages were short and clear-cut: just barely enough to understand what the messages were about, leaving no time at all for questions.

Anna had no doubt that this third message needed to be delivered to Mr. McDavid's wife. It was Anna who was destined to be at his deathbed, and she was the one who could receive his messages in dreams and relay them to Jennifer. Even with the spousal relationship and love bond, Mr. McDavid's soul was unable to contact his wife in dreams. It was Anna who was chosen to be the intermediary.

Having second thoughts about again telling Jennifer of her husband's coming to her in a dream, Anna called but altered the story slightly, saying that due to her absence of mind, she forgot one important message from Mr. McDavid to Jennifer before he died. Anna then repeated the message that was still vivid in her head.

Jennifer protested that she had already looked in her husband's blue folder. It was just a pack of old health records, and there was nothing else. Anna was very disappointed when hearing the immediate response from Mrs. McDavid, but having confidence in her dream, she persisted in encouraging her to double-check in case she might have overlooked something important. Anna then heard a long sigh, followed by the sounds of turning pages, and then silence.

Just over a minute later—though to Anna it seemed like an hour—she heard Mrs. McDavid utter, "Here it is." Then she cried aloud. Her weeping prevented her for a long time from telling Anna what she had found: a life insurance policy worth more than 1 million dollars, payable upon his death.

"Any more messages from her husband?" had been the last question in Anna's memory about this poor lady. Anna had prayed that Mr. McDavid's soul and his love would be always with his wife and daughter.

Anna intended to tell Mrs. McDavid the whole story if Mr. McDavid ever came into her dreams again. But he never returned. Anna guessed that all his attachments to this world had been undone and, his tasks completed, he'd be on the way to a new life in another realm—or busy watching over his wife and daughter.

CHAPTER 7
BACK TO THE LONELY JOURNEY

1

In her own personal life, her marriage to Mike was beginning to become more and more intolerable. Mike had intense mood swings. He blamed his wife for all of his failures. Mike was never able to find a job or complete any of the degrees he started, and Anna was the only income earner in the family. She also took care of the children and their home. The burden became unbearable.

Anna came home one morning after an exhausting night call at the hospital. She found her son in a dirty diaper and Mike still drunk from the previous night. The nanny had already left. This was the breaking point. She waited until Mike was sober and awake. At this juncture, she asked for a divorce. The thought of being trapped in this loveless and overwhelming marriage made her feel suicidal. If she continued on, her children would model this type of relationship, thinking of it as normal. There was no other way out. She wondered if she had ever loved Mike, a very intelligent man whom she met while in medical school. From the very beginning Mike was interested in her and helped her with schoolwork. Over time, closeness, respect, and friendship changed into a comfortable relationship. Anna had mistaken this for love.

Mike had been studying to become an electrical engineer before going to medical school. Actually, he did not want to be a doctor, but his father forced him into it. His father, a test pilot, was employed by an aircraft company. An aircraft he was testing, a light L-19 model, was flipped by strong, swirling winds and crashed to the ground, bursting into flames. He safely escaped but returned to rescue the copilot, who was entangled in the wreckage. The airplane exploded and killed the copilot. Mike's father was burned over 80 percent of his body and died a few days later.

Before the accident, Mike's father had maintained a close relationship with Anna. He often found time to invite her for lunch or dinner whenever she was not busy. Anna thought that his heroic act had influenced her to marry this man's son. Mike quit medical school right after his father's funeral, devastated by the accident and perhaps also driven by his dislike for the medical field. Mike inherited some money from his father's life insurance and later, very long after the marriage, Anna found out he had begun using drugs and was arrested once for forging narcotic prescriptions.

Mike's father had always been very fond of Anna. This could have stemmed from his previous love for an Asian girl, a Korean he met when he was in the Korean War. He told no one why he had not married this beautiful Korean girl, but he also never concealed his love for her from Mike's mother. This could have contributed to the permanent hatred Mike's mother harbored for Anna. She had even refused to come to her son's wedding, saying she was in poor health. Mike's mother fell deeper and deeper into heavy prescription-drug addiction and smoking. She died of an overdose at the age of sixty-one. Mike had hoped his mother would leave him some money, but she had none to leave, because she had spent it all.

Being broke and unemployed certainly affected Mike's behavior and attitude. Early on, he felt superior to his wife, being a white male, seeing himself as more intelligent. But now, he felt inferior: a parasite who lived by a female's support. He loved his children, but his indulgence toward them caused much family conflict: junk food and drink, no rules and regulations, no discipline for bad conduct, carelessness about obesity. Since he didn't work, he stayed home to feed the children and himself the way his mother had during his upbringing. They were constantly broke, because he spent all the money Anna had made.

Worse, he took personally almost everything that Anna said. He constantly complained about Anna having no respect for him. By the time Anna had asked for a divorce, there had been very little good communication between them.

Living with him or without him—which one would be better for her and the kids? Anna asked herself if she had ever really loved Mike or whether, like many other young people, she had been confused about the difference between "like" and "love" from the very beginning of their relationship. Mike was a man of self-respect, but not a good husband and father. He was right when blaming her for her disrespect; Anna had indeed lost confidence and respect for him because of his past involvement in drugs, which he had concealed from her. That could also be the reason he never got a job of any kind, no matter where he lived.

After considering all possible circumstances, Anna came up with her decision, the one that brought pain and shame to her, the children, Mike, and her parents as well: the decision to divorce. She might have saved them all this pain and shame if only she had listened to her grandmother's warning, she realized.

At the final hearing, Anna agreed to the court's order to provide spousal support of 7 percent of her income for thirty months. The divorce was finalized. Mike moved out and Anna began a journey in life with two children. After twelve years living as husband and wife with Mike, Anna realized she felt neither sad nor happy when he left the house. She only found indifference in her heart. There was a surprising feeling of lightness; after all, the burden had been lifted. If the children had not been around, she might have thought of her past marriage as no more than a dream.

2

Anna gave a lot of thought to love and happiness after the divorce. She was not sure whether she and Mike ever had real love for each other or whether there was happiness during their twelve years living as husband and wife. Perhaps divorce came as the result of a death of love, she thought. But what was love? In one sense, if love only meant the intense sexual desire for another person of opposite gender, then it would have a very short life. In this sense, love was not far away from lust.

Anna's father once told her that love took root from deep in one's heart and showed in the eyes. One's instinct could tell love or hatred displayed in another. Animals could do this, also. A sign of love between two persons would be a sense of missing the other when separated and of happiness when being together. He also reminded her that love dies rapidly after marriage if the partners do not nourish it carefully. There are differences of opinion on love between the East and West. Eastern love is introversive, as opposed to the extroversive idea of Westerners. Concerned about these differences, he encouraged his children to seek spouses of the same culture and race.

Happiness is another term much used in marriage. But now perhaps Mike was happy not to be in the marriage, and so was Anna. Then what is the real meaning of happiness? she wondered. She asked her father this question on of the day of her first wedding anniversary, when he wished her a full life of happiness. He gave her the answer, quoted from a European philosopher, that "she should expect something to come, not as she wants, but expect it to come as it comes. This is real happiness."

Anna once had a Vietnamese boyfriend, a college student in Manhattan, Kansas, when she was attending Saint Mary of the Plains. He lived in an apartment and gave Anna a key so she could stay there whenever she came to visit. One day Anna went to Manhattan for some school projects. Her boyfriend was either absentminded or careless about the key, because Anna opened the apartment and found he was with another girl. Not listening to his explanations, Anna backed out and never contacted him again. She felt betrayed by a man of her same race and culture. After that, she came to the decision that she would marry anyone she loved, regardless of race or culture, the same way she would treat patients of any race or culture as a physician.

It seemed strange to Anna that she felt better at home after Mike moved out. She felt free to say anything without worrying about offending him or hurting his feelings. She tried to keep everything as normal as she could. Not many people knew of her divorce, even at her workplace. She seemed more energetic and happier. She just wanted a peaceful life, body, and soul.

After having this peaceful life for about one year, Anna met a patient named Hugo, from Europe. Hugo came under her care by pure chance. He was assigned to her after being admitted for chest pain. After multiple evaluations, Hugo was found to have a disastrous diagnosis, a dissecting aneurysm that started at the base of this heart and extended vastly into his body. The hope of Hugo surviving this was next to impossible—and if he did survive, he would not have lived a normal life.

Hugo came to the United States as a real estate investor. He fell in love with the lake areas around Austin. Hugo's family started by buying some waterfront houses and land. Hugo lived in Austin permanently and worked as a project manager. Much of Hugo's business in the United States was directed by his family in Belgium. His father and Omer, his brother, were both civil engineers. Omer modernized his father's company and brought about growth and expansion. As an owner and CEO of an engineering and development company, Omer was contemplating additional investments in real estate, since the construction business seemed slow at that time. Though not very busy just then, he had to stay in Europe to take care of his business, only coming to the United States if the situation required.

Hugo's circulation was compromised by the dissecting aneurysm, and his blood pressure was increasing at an alarming rate.

Surgery was impossible because of the extensiveness of the dissection. Medicine was the only way to temporarily hold his blood pressure down in hopes of slowing down the dissection. It was the last effort. Hugo was still able to talk. Like most people from Belgium, he was fluent in five languages.

When Omer called and demanded his younger brother's status, Hugo assured him that his condition was not serious; he had just contracted the flu. But his unusual tone of voice and his stay in the ICU alerted his older brother that he was in danger. Omer took a flight to come see Hugo right away.

Hugo was receiving the maximum medical treatment possible, and it was expected to stabilize him only for a while. Despite much effort, Hugo slipped into a coma as the dissection worsened. One by one, his internal organs began to fail. Anna asked his family's permission to take Hugo off life support at this juncture. After two weeks, Hugo died in peace, in the presence of his brothers, Omer and Tony, and Anna. Hugo's body was cremated and transported back to Belgium and buried in his hometown cemetery.

Though in sorrow, Omer Verhaeghe felt that Hugo was lucky to have had Anna's care during the last two weeks of his life. Anna was surprised to learn that the family brought her gifts in appreciation for what she had done for Hugo. They came back again and again during the year, and Anna became very close to Omer and his family.

Omer was a divorced parent with two children. Since his divorce almost a decade earlier, he had shared custody with his former wife. As a civil engineer, he managed his business successfully and saved a large amount of money. When he perceived a decline in the European building business, he turned his interest toward real estate purchases in the United States, and he chose Austin, Texas, to be the pilot area for his plan. Omer was a typical European gentleman in the way he spoke, his manner, and the intimacy with which he greeted people.

While caring for Hugo, Anna did not pay much attention to Omer at first. At their first meeting, something extraordinary happened. Neither one could understand, at that time, what had transpired. As Anna walked into the ICU waiting room to meet with Hugo's family, Omer was waiting for her and politely said good morning and thanked her for being his brother's doctor. Anna was entranced and speechless when she looked at Omer. A priest and family friend who accompanied Omer that morning remarked how the room seemed silent and the world fell away, leaving only these two people present. Omer later recounted that he felt instantly enamored and disoriented at the same time. Something had happened in that instant and no one could explain it.

In their following encounters, Anna noticed several beautiful things about Omer. He possessed a gentle, deep look: full of intimacy for others that could pierce the heart. A smile appeared permanently on his face. He was very humble and respectful to everyone. Once in a while a sad look crossed his face, and then it dissolved into smiling again.

There was something unique about Omer and Anna's meeting. Some mysterious force pulled Omer nearer to Anna. He found that he could not stop thinking about her. He told his family about this woman that he could not get out of his mind. He told his mother, "This is a woman that I am going to marry. I knew that from the moment I saw her."

He found any opportunity to be with her. He brought Anna and her children precious gifts from Europe whenever he came to the

United States. He played with her children, helped fix things around the house, and made himself available if Anna needed him. He took any chance he could get to be with her.

They talked about everything. Anna once asked what he thought about the United States. Since Anna's career was in the medical field, Omer opined that he loved the United States, but worried about its health-care problems. Anna protested that America was considered to have one of the world's best medical systems; what could he possibly worry about? Omer pointed out that obesity would be the problem that brought the United States down. Currently, the obesity rate in children was past 40 percent nationwide, and it kept going up. Not very long in the future, Omer said, the United States would become a sick country instead of a strong one. More and more young people were fighting diabetes, high blood pressure, strokes, and so on. How would it be possible to build up a country with generations of ailing young people? he asked.

Anna had to agree with what he was saying. Omer had some knowledge in areas such as economy, finance, engineering, and, above all, cultures. Anna found several of his customs, food, and family matters were similar to hers. The more she talked to him, the more interesting she found him.

Omer continued to pursue her friendship but kept his true feelings to himself for quite a while. Their relationship came to a turning point after nine months. Omer invited Anna to have a dinner at a luxurious, quiet restaurant, where he reserved a private table for the two of them. Walking to the indicated seat, Anna felt at once that Omer was going to say something special. True to her expectation, over a glass of wine, Omer began his confession.

"I don't believe in love at first sight but knew instantly I loved you the first time I saw you. But, you were my brother's doctor. I had to focus on my brother. There were so many emotions as my feelings turned to sorrow when it dawned on me that my brother could not be saved. I loved my brother very much; I would have been willing to die in his place. As his older brother, I felt hopeless, unable to do anything for my own brother or even show him my love and compassion.

"For almost two weeks, I watched how you cared for my brother. You brought him everything: affection, compassion, sympathy, love, and, above all, comfort for his fear of an impending death. I saw a beautiful person underneath the image of a respected doctor.

"Having noticed my feelings for you, my father reminded me that my grandfather, whose name was also Omer, married a woman with the name Anna, my grandmother.

"For several months I have been neglecting my business in Europe, staying in the United States to be near you, to allow you to know more about me, and most of all, to see if you have any interest in me. I must go back to Belgium tomorrow. I would like to have peace of mind on the way home by knowing whether or not you have feelings for me."

Anna had been trying hard to hide her emotion while Omer spoke. She pretended indifference while listening to the words from his heart, but she was not at all surprised by Omer's confession, which confirmed what she had read from the way he looked at her and how he cared for her.

Neither in denial or acceptance, Anna asked him to give her more time to think it over. She had been divorced for just more than a year, she explained, and she was fearful because she did not want to make the same mistake again. She reminded him that they were both single parents who had children to care for. Both had tasted enough bitterness and sweetness in life. She had great affection for him, she said, but she needed more time to find out if she loved him and if he loved her. She asked him to give her two years. She felt that if his feelings remained the same in two years, they could start to plan a life together. Their love seemed impossible! Not only was there a racial difference (like her first marriage), but also they lived in two different countries! How was this going to work? It appeared that this relationship would be more challenging than the first.

That night, Anna had a dream in which she brought her two children to a park for a walk. While walking along a path of green grass, all three of them were suddenly lifted up and brought to a beautiful garden. Everywhere there were strange flowers that exhaled such wonderful fragrances. Birds of every color flew around to greet them. A sound of heavenly music was heard from far away in the sky.

During the moment of her wonder, Anna's children turned into angels and flew away. A few minutes later, they came back with another angel, who kept looking at her with eyes full of love. The new angel told her that she had been called to this place to meet him and stay with him. She should not go back to the transient mortal world full of sorrow and worries.

She wanted to heed him, because once leaving this place, she knew she would not be allowed to come back here again. But she replied to him that she must go back. She had patients and many other duties to fulfill, she said. People needed her in that world, not in this one. When she finished, instantly the new angel changed into Omer and his figure gradually faded away into the clouds.

Upon waking, Anna thought of her dream as a fairy tale her grandmother told her during childhood to lure her into sleep. It was about a young, beautiful girl rescued by a mandarin. She promised to return his favors one day. Being fed up with the troubled life of a mandarin, he resigned and went seeking beautiful scenes in mountains, creeks, trees, birds, and flowers, where he could compose poems and music. One day, while walking along the seashore, he saw magnificent mountains floating in the distance out at sea. Some mysterious voice called him from inside. He hired a young man to row a boat to the mountain, where he met the pretty girl he had rescued previously. The floating mountain was the sixth fairy world, where he was destined to meet his wife.

After living there about a year, he missed his home terribly and was determined to go back. His wife wept and told him that he could not come back to her once he left her. He was not convinced. His wife took her hairpin, blew her breath into it, and the pin changed into a flying object that carried her husband home. Like Rip Van Winkle, the mandarin could hardly identify his village, because one year in the fairy realm was equal to more than a hundred years in the earthly world. Realizing his desperate plight, the mandarin rushed back to his vehicle, hoping to fly back to his wife, but it had turned into a heavenly bird and flew into the clouds.

Crushed, he walked into the mountains, hoping to find a way leading to the fairy world. No one knew whether he died in the mountains or returned to his lovely wife.

When driving Omer to the airport, Anna planned to tell Omer of her dream, but she thought better of it. She reserved time and her keenest senses to find out how strong his love for her was. She did feel warm and sacred love from him on the way to the airport, and his eyes were still on her right before he slipped into the security gate.

Anna felt so lonely on the way back home. She really missed him and ached for his return. To others, Omer had seemed nothing special. But Anna felt like a thin piece of metal pulled by a strong magnet—Omer. From deep in her heart, Anna knew that she loved him and there was no question about it. She realized that she had never missed her ex-husband the way she already missed Omer. She could not believe that she could have a taste of love at more than forty years of age. This love had come unexpectedly, when she was not ready for it.

Also, she loved a man from a different race and a different continent. Her father was probably wrong to say that there was no real love between persons of different races. Was this love why she came to Austin, she wondered? Did poor Hugo have to die so that Omer could come to her? Was her love coming from death? If so, that price was terribly dear. She surmised that Omer was anxiously waiting for her answer, but she did not want to give it to him yet. She wanted to be a single parent for a while with her children. She was not ready for marriage yet. She was waiting for the thing that comes as it comes.

Before long, Anna received an invitation from Omer's parents for Hugo's anniversary celebration. Inside the envelope was a round-trip air ticket for her from Austin to Belgium. Anna was eager, but also hesitated to go. She anticipated that Omer would ask her again when she saw him face-to-face. But she went on with preparations to go. This was the first adventure she would take to Europe, the one that fate had set for her.

Everyone in Omer's family was very friendly and respectful to her as a doctor from the United States. At first, Anna did not know why she was invited for this occasion. She found out later there were a couple of reasons why she had been invited. First, beside Hugo's tomb, Mr. Verhaeghe, with one arm around Anna's shoulders and eyes full of tears, announced that he had lost a son but obtained Anna as a new daughter in return. Her presence would be a great consolation for the family. She would stand in Hugo's position so that there was no vacant seat in the house of Verhaeghe.

With deep emotion, Anna accepted this honor. With Mr. Verhaeghe's remarks, Anna saw herself at once as a member of the family. She was then widely introduced to almost the whole community as "Hugo's doctor, Anna, a Vietnamese," followed by the long recitation of all she had done in caring for Hugo before his death.

Anna blushed with pride. She humbly denied all credit that had been given her. Though proud to be praised as a Vietnamese, Anna gently corrected that she was a US citizen and was only born in Vietnam. That was the second purpose for which she was invited to Belgium. The Verhaeghe family showed love and affection to her, and she loved them, too. Anna went on a guided tour of Belgium. A small country, she saw most of it in a few hours.

The next day, Omer took Anna to France. After visiting museums and the Eiffel Tower, Omer cut the tour short to bring her to Luxembourg Gardens, where he hoped to have some private time with her. Walking along an alley, Anna had a sense that she had been here before. The road, rows of trees, and even the banks at the roadsides looked very familiar. She stood still and was deep in thought: "Have I been here before? No, I have never been in France, never in this garden."

Omer asked if there was something wrong, and she just shook her head in reply. Then she smiled when remembering her dream of more than three months ago. She wondered if it was a coincidence, or if her soul had been brought here during a dream. In her dream, her children and Omer were all angels, but she was not. Just then, Anna looked up and saw a statue of an angel at the road corner. Anna put both hands on her forehead and tapped it several times to see if she were in waking reality or still in a dream.

She sat on a stone bank and closed her eyes for a while. She could see that her dream might be trying to foretell something, but she was unable to figure it out. When she opened her eyes and looked up, the statue of the angel was there, and Omer, his eyes full of worry, was looking intensely at her. Anna's smile gave Omer a sigh of relief, and he sat down next to her. He put his hands behind her neck, gently pulled her closer, and kissed her.

They became lovers. Anna had gone a long journey to answer Omer. Both had found a love late in life. But, this time, it was a real love.

3

Back in Austin, Anna made plans to introduce Omer to her parents and siblings, and she had high hopes that they would all like him. In spite of her age and being raised in another culture, Anna remained a Vietnamese girl and needed to follow some Vietnamese customs and traditions. She regretted that she had disobeyed her parents in her marriage to Mike. It took a long time for her to make peace with them. Though pretty sure about her intuition this time, she still liked to see what her parents said about Omer before making any major decision.

She called her parents in Houston, saying she had found the man, another white man, from Europe; that she loved him; and that she wanted them to meet him. Her father was not really happy with the news. He seriously reminded her, "Real love is not easy to find. Most people when growing up anxiously jump ahead in the journey, searching for a real, ideal love in people of different races and cultures. They later find disappointment and deception instead. Not many discover real love, since real love virtually never exists. What people view as love is actually the desire for another. It fades away soon after the wedding. If it is a real love, then it never dies."

Having said that, Anna knew that her father had tried to avoid mentioning her last, failed marriage. He did not want to repeat the word "divorce," which still rankled in his heart. He was very pessimistic about family status in America. People said "I love you" when they did not mean it, he told her. Could a promise have any credit if it was said by a person who had vowed before God more than four or five times? Those were the things her father complained about.

Anna did not blame her father for his distressing criticisms, because he belonged to a different time and place. He was born in an area influenced heavily by Confucian principles. He was sent in his childhood to a school where he learned strict moral codes and had to pass difficult tests before being admitted into academic classes. These moral codes and principles took root in most countries of eastern Asia. But these basic conduct standards were destroyed by communism. Unfortunately, they were not observed in the West, either. Her father discouraged the intermarriage between East and West, stemming from his opinion that there were so many differences: culture, customs, traditions, religion, and so on. But the most important one was in the way of thinking and the philosophy of life. These differences could certainly affect the relationship between husband and wife.

As a daughter, Anna knew well her father's concerns, and she had prepared for that. From the early days of their acquaintance, she had brought up crucial issues in many conversations with Omer, and she was amazed and happy that Omer, though born and raised in the West, possessed the same cultural features as people from the East. That gave Anna so much confidence in introducing Omer to her parents. Anna perceived her father as a tolerant man and went ahead with her plan.

Having been disappointed with Anna's divorce from a man of different culture, her parents seemed skeptical and reserved when encountering the man she brought to their house in Houston. Her father repeated almost the same things that he had discussed previously with Mike, Anna's ex-husband. He emphasized the cultural differences and acceptance of each other. He reminded Omer not to expect Anna's nature to change, but to learn to accept her the way she was.

Omer voiced his agreement with what Anna's father had said. He proceeded to talk about himself, his family, his parents, and his business. He had had almost everything he wanted in life except a sincere love. He had found in Anna what he had always aspired to. He loved her not for how she looked or because she was a doctor; he loved the things deep inside her. He had come to her because he had heard her voice calling from a gentle, lenient heart. Most of all, Omer asserted that he came to Anna not by chance, but by predestined intention.

With sincerity, openness, and above all, similar moral principals in life, Omer won sympathy from Anna's father at the end of the day. As for her mother, Anna had noticed that she did not voice any opinion about Omer at all the whole time. She stayed calm and quiet and seemed reluctant to participate in conversations. But Anna didn't worry, because her mother showed no sign of hostility.

Anna and Omer were very happy about this successful meeting. On the way to Austin the next day, they discussed what they would do next. Actually, they knew what they were going to do, only they needed to decide how to do it more satisfactorily.

The evening came and it was a most beautiful and romantic one for them. Sitting on a pontoon on the lake in front of Omer's house, they related to each other the stories of the past: bad and good experiences they had been through, successes and failures they had endured, sorrows and happiness they wanted to share, the future family model they planned to build. Billions of bright twinkling stars were looking down on them and shed a milky, blurred light on the smooth surface of the lake. Trees around the lake seemed to be holding still to listen to the lovers' heartbeats. Wrapped in Omer's arms, Anna felt her youth return, a time that she had viewed as lost. She had not believed that she could love again until she met Omer. She forgot that it was late and that her two children were waiting to go home.

At home she found a message on her phone to call her mother as soon as she could. After putting the children to bed she came to her room, shut the door, and called her mother. It was late, but she knew her mother was waiting for her. As Anna expected, her mother picked up the phone right after the first ring.

Heaving a long sigh to open the conversation, Anna's mother asked if she really trusted and loved Omer. Anna confirmed her trust and love and asked her mother what her concerns were about him. She sighed again and told her daughter what was bothering her.

"No doubt that I like Omer. I like his manners, his personality. I like the way he talks, how he present his ideas, the honesty in answering your father's questions. He was polite, humble, and knowledgeable on many issues. He was also very considerate, the quality I like the most. He will be the perfect choice for a husband. But, there was something that I wish I knew how to tell you. Right from the very moment he walked into the house, I felt uneasy at once. When shaking hands with him, a cold stream ran over my body, though his hands were warm. When close to him, a fear overwhelmed me. During the time you and he were with us here, I stayed calm, trying to figure out what was wrong about him. I found nothing. Omer all the time was smiling and charming. That was all. I do not know; what do you make of it?"

Anna brushed off what her mother told her as race profiling and stereotypes resulting from her divorce from her ex-husband. She trusted her mother's intuition sometimes, but now, Anna thought, her mother's intuition had gone too far. She believed in her own feelings.

Exactly two years to the day they met and as he promised, without any formal ceremony, Omer brought a precious ring to put on Anna's finger and asked her to marry him. The ring resembled Princess Diana's engagement ring. Parents of both sides were informed of her acceptance and they proceeded to plan for the official engagement and wedding in the near future.

Anna was very happy with her decision. Her children loved Omer. They were in need of a father as a role model for their growing up. Omer was a good person who cared for and loved them as his own. She fell in love, enjoyed life, and was happier than ever.

After Omer's previous marriage failed, he lost his trust. His failed marriage brought dishonor, disgrace, and humiliation for him and his family. He gave up hopes of finding a happy ending. He spent his energy, instead, in his work and his company. It was not until he met Anna that there was a second chance for happiness. He had a sense of comfort and joy when he first saw her, even before she looked in his direction. Now, he had found his real happiness with Anna. Instead of hating his ex-wife, he silently thanked her for her departure from him to make room for Anna.

He told Anna of his thoughts. Anna remarked jovially that she favored more the word "love" than happiness, because love could be carried to wherever, even to the other world, as opposed to happiness, which existed only when together. Happiness would disappear once there was a separation.

Omer had planned their wedding for the early months of 2008. In June 2007, he considered buying and remodeling a closed restaurant in the lake area for the wedding reception. After the wedding, it would open to serve as a restaurant again for the local people and tourists. Meantime, they allotted their time for travel together as much as they could and forgot their troubled pasts.

Returning to Belgium, Omer perceived the decline of his business. He sold half of his engineering company to his employees and planned to move all his investments to the United States. He bought some more land and houses in Austin that he thought of as good deals. Being so in love, he was not aware that the housing and banking businesses were headed toward bankruptcy.

Until November 2007, he was still optimistic about his investments in the United States and planned to buy some more properties. Then some bad news came from home and he stopped everything, even postponing the wedding day to the next year. Omer became lost in thought most of the time. Something grave troubled him badly, but he did not reveal what it was. He still attended Anna's family's traditional reunion, held in Kansas City this time. For the first two days in Kansas City, he acted normally. But more news arrived on the third day that brought fear to Omer.

He avoided everyone and locked himself in a small room down in the basement. Anna worried, trying to find out what the news was about. Omer assured her it was merely some small matters at home, and he would fix them when he came back. Anna knew this was a lie. She sensed something terrible taking place in Belgium that worried Omer. He took neither food nor drink, just lay flat on the bed, staring at the empty ceiling, heaving constant sighs of despair. Anna wrapped up and left early in order for Omer to fly back home to solve his problems.

On the way to the airport, Omer seemed like he was in a dreamlike state. His eyes were distant and deep in thought. He even avoided answering Anna's questions. But when coming to Austin, Omer pulled himself together and smiled again. He apologized to Anna about his behavior. He then booked an air ticket to Belgium that very night, for his father wanted him home as soon as he could arrive. His good-bye embrace seemed so final.

Anna's phone began to ring constantly. Her family demanded

to know what had been the matter with Omer. They were all disappointed to hear her answer that she had no clue at all. She was waiting to hear from him. Twenty-four hours went by since he had reached Belgium, and there was little news from Omer. Another twenty-four hours passed and still there were only a few phone calls from him. This was very unusual, as Omer would text her constantly when he was away. At seven thirty a.m. on the second week of his return to Belgium, the last text appeared: "Please remember that I love you, not just in this lifetime, but forever. I can't do it anymore. Forgive me." The phone rang an hour later. But it was not Omer's voice. It was his father's. In a hoarse, weeping tone, he told Anna that Omer had ended his own life.

Anna was frozen at the news and lost her sense of reality for a while. She then murmured a word—"why"—not intentionally asking anyone. She heard the faint answer from the other end of the line: "I don't know," followed by weeping sounds. Anna collapsed on the nearest sofa and was unable to cry. She just sat with her mind blank.

She had no doubt that Omer was dead. Hope, happy times, the future, peace of mind, promises of a life together—all of them had followed Omer into the other world. Anna kept wondering why and why again and again. What was it that he must die for? Why did he not tell her anything at all of why he had sacrificed his life? Would she have the right to know his secrets? Thousands of questions tortured her mind during the night and would probably continue for the rest of her life if they were not answered properly.

The next call in the morning from Belgium informed her that a letter from Omer for his parents and for her was found, and they asked if she could come to Belgium. They wanted to open the letter in her presence. Her immediate answer was yes, for the reason that Anna hoped she could find the cause for his fatal decision once she read the letter or spoke to someone in his family.

John, a young man living in Austin and a friend of Omer's family, called and told her that Omer's parents had asked him to accompany her to Belgium.

Anxious to read the letter, Anna and John flew to Belgium on the earliest flight she could get. Waiting for them at the airport was Omer's father. At the door of the airport, Omer's father, William, rushed to Anna, embraced her, and cried uncontrollably. In crying, he kept mumbling, "He took my place. I should die in his place. I am an old and useless man."

Omer's family uttered a wailing sound in unison when seeing Anna. They dragged themselves to her and the three of them held tight together and wept silently. Their shoulders shook constantly with sorrow and affliction.

Omer had brought his death mystery to his grave. There was no letter specifically for Anna. In the envelope, only one letter was found in which he wrote to his parents and also to Anna. For Anna's part, he simply confirmed his love for her and asked her for forgiveness. That was all, nothing else. Nothing indicated why he had hung himself. No one told her anything, but looked at her with tears in their eyes.

Everyone tried not to even mention his death. Anna's loss and sorrow were deep and seemed insurmountable; it had caused a wound in her heart that would never be healed. During the funeral, Anna was not in sadness or sorrow. Instead, she was numbed and shocked that he had betrayed her completely. He did not tell her or share with her anything that resulted in his death. His business in Europe was perhaps going down, but not to the point that he must kill himself.

Numbness and shock were replaced by intense pain and anger. Anna was also angry that he had just destroyed the trust in him that she had begun to build. His death might somehow save his secret, if there was one, but it would leave her a life full of questions, desperation, and anger. She felt that not only did he have no respect for her but also he lied to her when he had said that he loved her. He did not love her at all. How could someone be in love and take his life? It did not make any sense. If he did, he must know how much she would endure because of his death.

And then, in the next moment, Anna told herself that Omer did love her. Thinking of all that Omer had said and done, she still contended that he was very sincere in his feelings for her. She trusted her instincts that he was not lying or saying what he thought she wanted to hear. When he spoke, she felt his compassion, emotion, and love generated through his eyes and moody face. Anna came to defend him; there must be something very grave that Omer was unable to disclose to her. And so it goes over the next few months. Anna would move through different stages of grieving.

After the funeral, Anna decided she must contact Omer one way or the other. If a dead man inside an elevator or in a dream could talk to her, and if a spirit could rescue her from a wreck, then why could she not speak with Omer? He must explain to her why he did it, why he deserted her at the moment she thought was the happiest in her life. He had betrayed and left her without considering her suffering. She would never forgive him for this. She must see him before coming back to the United States. She had to have an explanation.

However, she did not know how to get to him. No one could help her with this. She needed a plan and carried it out all by herself for the next three days before leaving for the States. Her physician friends had volunteered to cover her leave for one week to mourn him. Now the anger had pushed her to use the rest of the week, trying to meet a dead man.

First, she thought about going to his tomb, but viewed it as dangerous to be at a strange place alone at night. Several other problems arose: how to get there alone, when to arrive, how long to stay to wait for him, whether he would appear, and what time and how to get back.

Second, in desperation, Anna thought about meeting a psychic. There were many of them in the United States, but how could she find one in this faraway land? She had read many stories about psychics before and she had generally been neutral, neither quite believing in nor denying them. When she was in Vietnam during the charity trip, she was very surprised that Vietnamese communist-atheist officials not only believed in psychics, but also asked psychics to contact the dead soldiers who had perished on the way to the South on the Ho Chi Minh Trail along the Laotian border from the North to the South. The psychics found them all, and their families brought their remains back to the village cemeteries. The communist government even officially set up an organization to conduct research about psychic work.

Two other authentic psychic stories had taken place in families related to her parents in Vietnam. These had made Anna wonder, but they were unknown to the world because either no one paid any attention to stories from small countries or there was nobody to write about them.

The person involved in the first story related to a girl and her mother. A young girl escaped the communist oppression by boat in October 1982. Until 2001, her parents did not hear anything from her. Hoping that she might still be living somewhere, they sought psychic help. One person gave them the phone number of a psychic in Saigon, the old capital of the Republic of South Vietnam. The lost girl's parents called the psychic whom they never saw and asked about their daughter. After acquiring enough information, the psychic told the girl's parents that their daughter was dead and buried on the beach of a small island. The psychic went on to tell them to go to the island to look for a man that the psychic described in detail. The girl's parents then gathered a group of three men and a young lady to go to the indicated place. The group found the described man, who admitted knowing where he had found the girl and buried her. He added that the girl had a red shirt on when he found her drifting toward the beach. The girl's parents confirmed the shirt their daughter had worn on the day of her departure. The man led the group to the beach. After carefully observing the surroundings, he pointed at one spot that he thought was the place of the girl's grave. The men dug deep and found nothing at that place. They called the psychic again, more than three hundred miles away, and reported to him that they had found the man he described, that the man had shown them the place to dig, but that the body of the dead girl was not there. The psychic, either with eyes that could see more than three hundred miles or having a Google screen in front of him, called the young lady in the group and told her to begin walking backward until the psychic ordered her to stop. He then asked the men to dig at the spot the young lady stopped. They dug and found the girl's body; a red nylon shirt positively identified it. Later, her parents found out that she was drowned trying to escape a man in the group who tried to rob her of the money and gold she had brought along.

A more recent psychic story Anna knew of was told by a communist family living in Hanoi, the capital of the Socialist Republic of Vietnam. This family was related to Anna's father and had a family member in the United States as a foreign-exchange student. Originally, this family was a patriotic one whose members enthusiastically joined the waves of people fighting for the independence of Vietnam in 1945, during and after World War II. They ran after Ho Chi Minh, a communist who painted himself as a patriot. A few months after the outbreak of the war, the oldest son among the fighters went missing and was never heard from again. His wife stayed single, waiting for him or at least wanting to know where he had been buried. In April 2006, following the instructions of a psychic, his remains were found at a mass grave containing six skeletons. Before digging, the psychic had mentioned the number of skeletons and the position of each, then specially pointed out the one that family was looking for after sixty years. The missing man was found, but it was too late for his wife, who had already joined him in the other world.

As she considered psychics, Anna viewed it as impossible to find one in Belgium, and she dared not ask for one. But if she could find one, she would go ahead and ask for help, regardless of what people thought of her. The only person she could express her ideas to was

John, her companion from the States. But when she mentioned it, he just shook his head in protest.

Anna then thought about the Ouija board. But just as with a psychic, she was unable to have it at once. She might do it later, in the United States.

At last a bold idea came to her: she would sleep in the room where Omer died.

When she requested this, Omer's father protested strongly at first, saying that he did not want her to be alone during this horrible time, but Anna persisted in her demand, insisting that she had to leave Belgium soon. Omer's father gave in at last to let her do as she liked. Out of worry for her safety, he asked John to sleep in a room close by to check on her in the night. Someone asked if she would be scared, being alone in that tragic room. Yes, she replied, if this were with a strange person she never knew, but with Omer, why should she be afraid? Besides, during medical school, she had dozed off in the morgue many times at night alone, and never did any restless soul come to bother her.

Anna walked in the room at about nine thirty, and it was very cold. She looked at the thermostat and it was set at only twenty degrees Celsius: about sixty-eight degrees Fahrenheit. Anna raised the room temperature to twenty-four degrees. Anna walked around to have a good look at everything. It appeared that no one had come to this room after Omer's death. The things were as Omer had neatly arranged them: clothes were folded, books were in line on the shelves, the desk was clean, file folders were arranged in their drawers, pictures of family and other individuals hung on the walls. There was nothing unusual about the room. She walked to the bed and told herself, "This is his bed." There was no trace of the body having lain on the bed sheet. Omer might not have slept on the night he took his life.

Anna sat in an armchair and waited for a long time. It was dark and quiet outside. Once in a while, John tried to make a pretend cough to let her know that he was there. Though staying calm, she still jumped at any noise coming from outside of the house. She had a feeling that he would come, but in which way and what shape, she did not know.

She waited and waited and she became very tired. She lay down on his bed, staring at the ceiling as she waited, and slowly fell asleep. A noise woke her suddenly. She ran to the window where the noise came from and found the window still closed, but it had been struck by a tree branch in the strong wind of a storm. It was about three o'clock in the morning. The rain then followed the storm.

She sat sill and thought about Omer. She wondered if she really loved him. Where was he now? Did he know that she was waiting for him here in his own room? She wanted him to embrace her as he used to. She heard a sound at the door and thought it was him. No, something was blown at the door by the wind. A sound like walking feet came from the yard, and again she hoped it was him. No, it was leaves swirling on the ground. She kept looking toward the door, hoping for him to appear. No, he was not there. She cried quietly in the night. Never in her life did she feel lonelier than at that moment. She sat up and waited again until dawn. "He didn't come," she told John when he came to take her to breakfast.

In the morning, everyone expected her to stop her craziness of sleeping in that room, but she announced that she would try one more time.

4

The second night Anna came earlier, and John was sent to the same nearby room to keep an eye on Anna. There was no rain or storm, but it seemed colder outside. Anna also felt more peaceful this night. She determined that she would go back to the States the next day whether Omer came or not. She announced in the dark, as if speaking to Omer, that her relationship with him would be cut off entirely if he chose not to come. She then calmly sat down on a bed and began to read.

About eleven p.m. she heard John calling her. "Did you call me, Anna?"

"No, I did not."

"These old homes. They make a lot of sounds," John said and went away.

He went back to his room; then, about twenty minutes later, he came and asked again the same thing. Anna had no idea why anyone would be teasing him so. John seemed puzzled and then deep in thought as he walked back to his room. Anna did not know what he was thinking or what he had made of all this.

About thirty minutes after John left, Anna heard talking. It was a faraway conversation among many persons. The sound of the voices came closer and closer to her room. Anna listened, trying to know what the voices were talking about, but she could not figure out what language the conversation was in. It was not English, and she had no idea who they were or where they came from. Though unable to understand their strange conversation, she was sure that their voices were very sweet, happy, and attractive. The voices became louder and louder.

At that very moment, a beam of light appeared at the door, and from out of that beam Omer walked toward her. Anna became numb. She had almost given up hope that he would appear at all and now here he came, earlier than she had expected. He was not an angel, not a ghost, just Omer walking. He seemed distressed. He came to sit beside her and embraced her. Strangely enough, his touch had almost a vibrational feel. From his arms a source of warmth, comfort, and love went into her body. Anna even felt his weight on the bed when he sat down.

The room was very noisy. Anna heard conversations in the background, as if there were many people in the room greeting one another. She clamored to begin her questions. He asked her to let him talk because he feared he may not have much time. There was urgency in his voice.

"While I am here, please do not say anything; just let me talk, because I have not much time with you."

"I can hardly hear you. Why is there so much noise?" she asked.

"I am not here alone. The noises come from those whom I bring with me to give me the energy that enables me to come to you in person. This may be the last time we can meet. It takes too much energy to be here. That is why I could not come to you last night, though I knew you were waiting for me."

"Why? Why?" was all she could mutter.

"I made a mistake. I had made some calculations, and I just made a mistake. I'm sorry. I am okay, honey; I am okay. Once my soul was liberated from my body, I was free of any pain or hurt or bad feelings from this material world. Please forgive me. Please forgive me. I still love you as ever."

His voice seemed weaker and weaker, gradually fading away as his figure became blurrier and blurrier. At the same time, a faint noise came back from afar for a few seconds, and it was completely silent afterward.

For a very long time, Anna just sat there with her mind blank. She could see and hear nothing.

Alone again in her room, Anna tried to refresh her memory of all that she had seen and heard. She came to the view that Omer seemed happy and free of pain and suffering. That removed her from the fear and worry that the soul of the suicide was cast into hell as was taught by the Church. Furthermore, she saw light around him when he came to the door and felt the warmth from his arms, indicating that he was not coming from hell at all.

This would likely be the last time that she could see him, as he had told her. The thought of never seeing him again made Anna so sad and lonely at that moment. She called out to him, "Omer, why have you come to me and dragged me into your life? Now, you are gone and free of all anxieties, worries, and sufferings, but you have left behind grief, sorrow, and disappointment for everyone. As for me, you destroyed my hope and broke my heart, and you took with you my happiness. I wish that I had never met and loved you."

Anna sat still on the bed. A coldness and loneliness enveloped her. Her wet eyes stared blankly through a window into the dark night.

Anna wanted to leave Belgium as early as possible to avoid more sorrow and grief in the family, because she could not prevent Omer's parents from crying whenever they saw her. His mother repeated again and again in tears that Anna had brought smiling and joy to her son, and he gave her sorrow and tears in return. It was not fair for Anna, and that made his mother cry miserably. When they cried, Anna cried with them.

In the afternoon, Anna went to Omer's tomb to say good-bye. She told him that she was going to leave for the United States the next day. She had no time to mull over what he had told her in the night, but she forgave him and still loved him as ever. Her love that he had brought with him to the other world would become an eternal one.

John had heard about the events of the night before from Anna and he knew that Anna had really met Omer in the night. He then resolved that it was no doubt Omer who had called him twice that night.

The news of Omer's death was a big blow to Anna's family as well. No one ever thought this misfortune would happen. Everyone loved him. In a very short period of knowing them, Omer had earned the trust, sympathy, and acceptance of all her family members. Anna's parents were very fond of him. They were glad that Anna had found the right man after all. They counted and waited for the day of their daughter's wedding. It was a shock for them, hearing the bad news. They did not trust their ears and wondered how a man who was smiling and happy all the time like Omer could kill himself so suddenly. What was it that he must die for? Why?

When returning from Belgium, Anna was asked by everybody the same question again and again: Why did he do it? Then there were speculations of motives such as business failure, bankruptcy, economic downfall, and even a family feud. Anna knew none of the above was true. What was it that was more important than anything else in the world that he needed to sacrifice his life for? What was it that outweighed his responsibility with his children and his family's reputation? What was worth risking excommunication from the Church? Anna felt still very offended and unable to have a moment of peace if she did not know why.

Anna concentrated her thoughts, reflecting on all she could remember since the first time she had come to know Omer, to see if anything provided a clue. Thinking about her time with him and going through all of his pursuits, what he said, his sources of income, and his investments, Anna was unable to find anything illegal. She trusted her intuition that he was an honest man, and she never had any suspicions about his business or his honorable love for her. Unable to ask anyone for information, Anna dug into all the emails he had sent her; she had printed out and tucked them into a folder in chronological order. Again, she found nothing suspicious.

Though unsatisfied in her research for the reason behind Omer's death, Anna forgave Omer, based on the words of Omer's soul—"I had made some calculations.... Forgive me. I still love you as ever"—and she believed that he had died for some cause more sublime than the love of hers and his children's. She then felt at peace and accepted what fate had reserved for her: incomplete love all the rest of her life. Her marriage was ended by differences; her true love was terminated by a sudden death.

Bringing back her memories from the moment before meeting with Omer's ghost, when in a state of anger, she had forgotten to ask what she really wanted to. When she saw him walking from the beam of light, her fury disappeared and she was so glad that he had come. A wave of vibrations went through her body when he laid hands on her shoulders. Omer might have spoken to her through telepathy, but his sweet voice sounded to her exactly as it did in his life. It was too bad that her time with him was so short and that she just passively listened to him without being allowed to ask any questions. Then he was gone.

When she came back to the other room, anger followed sorrow—not toward Omer, but at herself for not asking anything about his life in the other world. All her waiting for him only turned out to confirm what she already knew. She had earlier regretted that if she had been alert enough, she might have prevented him from dying. Now her regret seemed unjustified, because his death was apparently a must. It suddenly dawned on her that Omer often told her he was not afraid of death, because everyone must die at the end. He also teased her that doctors tried to cure patients' illnesses to postpone their deaths for some five or ten years. How long would ten years be compared to eternity?

Anna then remembered her mother's warning when she met Omer in Houston that there was something strange about him. Anna wondered whether Omer had died a long, long time before she met him, before he came to her parents' house. Now, she harbored no anger toward him. She still loved him, and her love would become immortal because he had carried her love to a holy realm. What Anna did not realize at that moment was that Omer's death would propel her onto a path that she did not initially want to go, her spiritual path. Over the next few years, she would inhale books regarding NDEs, hoping to understand death and life after death. The hunger and thirst to learn about this realm enveloped her.

5

Anna had no hope of meeting Omer again due to the lack of energy, as he explained it. But Anna was very sure he had stayed somewhere in a realm not far away from the earth where she could contact him in other ways. For a few months, without any sign of Omer around, not even in her dreams, Anna conceived that he might detach himself from this bodily world to go into a heavenly realm. She made a great effort to come back to routine daily work as a physician and as a mother of two children. She had tried not to think of or mention him.

It seemed to Anna that he continued to care for her more than his blood, his children. Anna again thanked him and wanted him to know that he owed nothing. He should be on his way, for she could take care of herself.

She wanted to go back to her life before meeting Omer. However, she knew that her life was not the same since his death. The pain of loss was still immense and unremitting. She thought often of the life beyond this bodily world and wondered what the plight of Omer's soul would be. How long could he be around her in this world? Would he need anything from her, such as prayers? What would her prayers for him be about? Where did he stay and who were the people he stayed with? If he wanted to be with her, did he need to have permission from God?

She knew he had been around her since she came back from Europe. Both she and her sister, Linh, saw him at her house on the same night only ten days after she came home from Belgium. Her sister cared and worried that Anna would be lonely, devastated, and sorrowful as result of Omer's death and, in turn, careless for the children. Linh came to stay with her for a week and insisted on sleeping on a sofa downstairs while Anna and the children stayed in their own room upstairs as usual. During the night, Linh woke up and sensed someone in the house. She saw a blurry shadow of a man at the stairs that disappeared quickly.

In the morning, Linh told her sister she thought Omer had been at the house during the night. Anna answered her sister, "He was here last night. I heard his voice but didn't see him."

Omer was not seen or heard of after that. Even on his anniversary, he was unable to come to her when she slept in his bedroom. Anna did not expect to encounter him, either, as he had already told her that it took too much energy for him to make an apparition. Besides, Anna wanted her life back as a mother and a physician. She wanted him to know that he owed her nothing and she wished him well on the way to a different world.

Almost two years after Omer's death, the weather turned bitterly cold as Anna prepared for Christmas 2010. One weekend, a friend invited her to an Asian restaurant for a year-end dinner. During the meal, she noticed a middle-aged lady who kept looking at their table. Anna thought that the lady might have misidentified her as an acquaintance. Sensing Anna's discomfort, the lady walked to Anna's table to identify herself as Roberta Rowen, an elementary school teacher. Mrs. Rowen then asked if Anna had time to hear a message for her from a young man. The lady then gave Anna a piece of paper on which she just jotted down her hotel room and phone number, and then smiled as she left the restaurant.

Anna would later learn that Mrs. Roberta Rowen, a well-known psychic from Denver, was passing through Austin and had met Anna at the restaurant by chance. She left the restaurant in haste and did not allow Anna enough time to ask about the identity of the man and the content of the message. Spurred by curiosity about who the young man could be, Anna was determined to hear the message. She called and got directions to the hotel. It took Anna about twenty minutes to get to Mrs. Rowen's place. It was cold and dark outside.

Anna was invited to sit on the sofa next to the lamp table. Being aware of the weather and the time of night, Mrs. Rowen went straight into conversation. She told Anna that she was a psychic, and once in a while a soul from another world contacted her, asking her to deliver a message. At the restaurant where they met, she was approached by a man named Omer Verhaeghe who wanted to tell Anna that he loved her and that Anna should look for a sign that informed her of his presence. That was all, and Roberta Rowen had nothing else to say. Anna thanked Mrs. Rowen and drove home.

Anna waited for Omer's sign. For the next three days, she could not find anything that indicated a hint of him. The fourth day, driving home in the evening, Anna found something tangled in her left foot. She reached and grabbed a bird feather, very white and resembling some she had collected in a box at home. She put the feather in her pocket and saved it in the box. The next day, a feather came again and stuck at her left foot at the same section of the road as the previous day. At that moment, she knew Omer's sign was a feather. Instantly, she realized why he had chosen the feathers.

It was because of an interesting incident that happened one month after Anna came back from Hugo's anniversary. On that morning, Omer came to her house to fix a leaking water line. After more than an hour, he heard a flapping noise inside the house. Checking it out, he found a small, beautiful white bird in the house. He thought the bird sneaked in through the door left ajar when he was in and out of the house several times. He was going to chase the poor bird out, but then a funny idea popped up. He would keep the bird inside, waiting for the kids to come home from school, and let them catch it and then release it for fun. The children did have fun luring the bird into a small room and used a net to catch the pitiful animal. They delivered the bird to Omer to set it free at the door. The poor bird flew away, but returned the favor by leaving three white, beautiful feathers in Omer's hands. When Anna came home later and was told the whole story, she protested to Omer that it was not a good a idea to imprint into the children's head a cruel act against animals. Omer replied that he just wanted to give the kids a little fun, that's all. He did not mean harm to the bird or to keep it in a cage. Anna then apologized for being too harsh. Later, Omer told Anna he loved her even more for her compassion, not only to human beings, but to animals as well.

Omer told the children that they must save the three feathers, because the bird left exactly three: one for John, one for Emily, and one for Anna. He said to the children, "These feathers are magical! For as long as you keep them, their magic will keep you safe and look after you. The bird may be gone, but his loyalty and love now lies with you for as long as you have them. Keep the feathers safe, especially when I am not here with you. The feathers will protect you." The children ran to find boxes to keep the feathers safe. Anna rolled her eyes at Omer for telling them nonsense, but he just smiled.

From this incident, a feather suddenly became a symbol of love for Omer and Anna. Gradually, she then forgot about feathers and the love symbol of Omer until they came back to her at this moment. When the feather appeared, part of her thought it must be a sign of Omer's presence. Another part assigned it to coincidence. She was not sure and needed further evidence.

One windy day, Anna gave a ride to another physician, Patricia Harris. In their conversation on the way home, she talked to Patricia about the feather story and how she thought it might be a sign that Omer used to inform her about his presence. Patricia smirked and ridiculed Anna for a nonsense belief. Before Patricia could go to her next opinion, a feather flew and stayed on the windshield right in front of her. Anna pulled the car to the shoulder, picked the feather, and showed it to Patricia. She then wondered how a feather could stay on the windshield against such a strong wind. Patricia turned to stare at Anna. She did not voice any more opinions, but her eyes looked from side to side to see if she could spot Omer.

As for Anna, she recognized without a doubt that the feather was a sign of Omer's presence around her. This was the sign in the message that the psychic had delivered to her. The feather as a sign brought Anna both joy and sadness: joy for the fact that Omer was still around her and had great love for her, an ideal love, as he had said when she missed catching the feather. It seemed that Omer's soul stayed as romantic as ever in the life beyond. As for the sad part, the sign told her that Omer was no longer able to contact her directly, even in dreams. He must go through other channels such as psychics to give her the messages, because too much energy was required for other methods. Anna wondered what she could do to help him with that. Would prayers do any good? Anna often believed that praying sent energy to anyone who was in need of it, for healing or for any other matter. She thought that praying was less ritual or a request for God to perform miracles, but rather more energy, and the more people to pray, the better. She promised to pray much more for him.

6

Omer continued to show his presence by sending a feather once in a while. Anna had to admit his love for her, but she was very concerned that because of her, or perhaps her love for him that bound him to this world, his soul might be stuck and unable to move on to a better realm.

What could she do to undo all his obligations? Where did his soul dwell, a pleasant place or an unhappy one? Was he confined or did he volunteer to be there? How much longer would he be there? What were his daily activities and under what set of rules and regulations? Was he free to come to her anytime he wanted?

Of course, there were no answers for these questions and Anna knew it. Since Omer's death, she had read book after book, hoping to discover some answer, anything at all to know Omer's plight in the other universe. Certainly, she did not disbelieve in life after death. But she wanted to know where life after death would drive a soul to, especially someone like Omer, who had died a violent death that was condemned by the Church.

Reflecting back on her very first experience with the Ouija board, Anna could not dismiss the existence of communication between the living and the dead. A wandering soul needed energy from three or four people to move the indicator from letter to letter to form an answer. There was not much information to be gained about the other world from the spirits. Either they were not allowed to reveal anything, or their knowledge was limited. The danger of the Ouija board was that there were also bad wandering spirits who would harm the players by sucking energy out of their bodies. As a result of energy loss, players could sicken or die.

Anna learned that the out-of-body soul described by Dr. Dexter, her professor at Saint Mary of the Plains, was not a new phenomenon. Those who practiced meditation and cultivated their abilities for months and years were able to send their souls out of the body at will. The soul was attached to the body by a type of invisible, vibrating string that guided it back to the body. This line is severed only at death.

This connecting line was still operative for people having a near-death experience, which is similar to an out-of-body experience. The soul was separated from the body but still linked to it by the connection, and the scenes of NDE episodes were taken from what was formed in their consciousness previously, Anna learned. However, NDE persons only reported what they experienced at the invisible line between life and death; they had no specific information about the path of the soul beyond the boundary line.

Anna discovered that apparitions in human form, such as Mr. Gordon in the hospital elevator in Kansas City, were quite rare. As Omer informed her, too much energy was needed to reclaim the person's image, or even a bird shape, like that used by Mrs. Johnson. Such apparitions can go through the walls or a mirror; they are no longer normal bodies of this world. Energy to perform such apparitions could be attracted from those who were willing to help. Omer had borrowed energy from souls he brought with him to meet Anna, but she had no idea of the nature of the relationship between Omer and these other souls. Nor did she know where Omer returned to when he left her.

Messages in dreams were the most common, in Anna's experience. She had come to believe that her soul could communicate with others of the same frequency or spiritual wavelength. She also realized that whenever she encountered difficulties, her grandmother always reached her in dreams, either giving solutions or consoling her. Her grandmother never mentioned anything about her life beyond, either.

Reflecting on what had been taking place, it appeared to Anna that both the dead and the living shared the same universe, but in a different state: seen and unseen. The universe of the dead and the invisible roads leading to this universe remained a mystery and Anna wanted to know more about it.

Based on all these facts from her own experiences, Anna strongly believed that there was no doubt about life after death, but what would be next? Christianity promised a heavenly reward for good souls and hell for the bad ones. However, she wondered if what was conceived as right or wrong in this world would be the same or different in God's judgment? What would right and wrong look like in heaven and hell? Were there any activities there? Could a soul advance to a higher and higher position in heaven? Are there different levels of reward in heaven? What does a soul get after being canonized by the Church—a higher position, or something else? Or did people reach the same level in heaven, no matter what good works they did?

As for the souls in hell, were they allowed a chance to redeem their past mischief so that they would be able to advance closer to God? Buddhism alone believed in a cycle of reincarnation, but no religion ever mentioned activities of the souls once entering the holy realms. However, Mysterious Original Divinity (MOD) contends that the life beyond is not very different from this world. There is no heaven or hell, but each soul was placed at a precise position in the other realm once leaving this earthly world. This position would be given according to the merit cultivated in life, and each soul continued its work to advance to a higher level. The level after death would be closer and closer to God, depending on the merits of the soul, and farther and farther into the darkness for wrongdoers. The ancient sages of India maintained that after this physical world, a soul would come to a level where it could go to and from this world if necessary. After completing all unfinished business related to living relatives, the soul advances to the higher level of consciousness and gradually to eternity.

Once going into eternity, what would be the relationships of soul to soul, children to parents, between siblings, and between the soul and God? Would each soul be given the same level of bliss? Is heavenly bliss the same as that of this world, or different?

Anna was not confident of anything in this world. Why did God want her in this world? Was it a blessing or a curse? Were her decisions made with her free will or by destiny? Had God dictated all the important events of her life: birth, marriage, number of children, divorce, and death? Christianity confirms God's decision on everything, even the fall of a hair from a human head. And the ancient Chinese agreed that each moment of drinking and eating had been determined by God. Hinduism's four principals of spirituality seemed to advise one to accept life as it had been destined:

1. Whomever you encounter will be the right one.

2. Whatever happened would be the only thing that could happen.

3. The moment in which something begins would be the right moment.

4. What is over is over.

As a physician, Anna realized that she might keep a life going a little longer, but she was ultimately powerless before suffering and death. A birth is a miracle, a wonderful mystery, but life lasts only a short time. In death or passing over, beautiful life creations are destroyed mercilessly. Suddenly, she was skeptical of her role as a doctor. She had lost confidence and direction in life.

While in this confused mood, Anna was visited by Ann, Omer's sister, who Anna had met a couple of times in South Africa and in Belgium, and Ann's husband, Murray. Murray and Ann spent time discussing the unanswered issues facing Anna. Realizing that Anna was in need of help to find peace in her life, Ann asked Anna to consider meditation. It might not answer all her questions right away, she told Anna, but at least she could accept things as they had been happening, and peace would ensue immediately.

Ann then shared that she and Murray had been in meditation for some years. Murray had stopped after becoming very preoccupied with his business, but she kept practicing meditation daily. She told Anna that in the meditation process, peace for the mind is gained by overcoming worry. There is no more fear of death, because death only means that the soul leaves the body to a better realm. Anna thought of the piece of paper the Buddhist monk had shown her, on which he divided existence into Previous, Now, and Afterlife, separated by two lines. She remembered his words that there was no such thing as death. What people thought of as death was just a passing over of the next line. This could explain why Omer had ended his life easily. Ann also revealed that she sought meditation after enduring a tragic event in her own life.

Ann's advice reminded Anna of a Korean vet, also a patient of hers in Kansas City some years earlier. This patient, Kenneth Fulton, found meditation as a means to achieve peace of mind and remove his fear of dying.

Observing Anna's deep depression, pain, and grief continue, Anna's colleagues had suggested antidepressants and tranquilizers. "There has to be a better way," Ann thought, "than to numb the mind with all of these drugs."

Anna was determined to follow the path of meditation as Ann suggested. Pain visited her daily: a deep ache in her chest that was present every waking second. The only relief from this pain was sleep; a few seconds after awakening it quickly returned as the reality hit her.

As her pain continued on a daily basis, Anna was introduced to Art of Living, an international institute for meditation that had a branch in Austin, Texas. From childhood, she had associated meditation with Buddhism, a practice reserved for the Buddhist monks who sit in a lotus position for hours in the temples. She attributed it to the Buddhist way of praying. But now, Anna found meditation not to be Buddhist prayers, but the way to bring a soul near to God. Meditation, she learned, had become very popular among all beliefs.

Anna heard of a Korean Catholic priest who went back to a Buddhist pagoda in South Korea to meditate with Buddhist monks for two months. He announced that meditation helped him to meet with the Holy Spirit. Another white American Catholic priest had met with the Dalai Lama to learn about and discuss meditation. He, too, declared that meditation was the best way to pray and connect with God. He also encouraged people to come back to the old traditional way of praying, mainly concentrating the mind to be with God. Equipped with such information, one morning Anna came to meet the people at Art of Living in Austin.

True to her expectations, Anna met all kinds of people of different beliefs: Catholic priests and nuns, Buddhist monks and nuns, Baptist ministers, rabbis, and so on. There were also many young people of all races who came here either to seek God or to discover their spiritual identity. Anna was here to look for peace of mind. She participated in sessions twice a week for the first month and once a week for the second month, due to heavy work at the hospital.

For the first session, Anna was encouraged to be aware of two aspects: the outside and the inside. The outside part was her surroundings, and the inside part was the mind and its inner environment. The mind would stay peaceful if there were no intervention whatever from the outside surroundings, she was told. Meditation was the process of keeping the mind away from outside commotion. In order to ignore the outside completely, one must focus on something such as God, Jesus, Buddha, or Mohammed, and so on. In the third meditation session, for the first time in months, the deep pain in Anna's chest finally lifted.

It was easy for Anna at the onset to bypass everything from her surroundings, but it was difficult to avoid various kinds of thinking and complexity in her mind. With help from a guide, gradually she was successful in the process. Once she was oriented in the right way, she found peace of mind. Sorrow, sadness, and negative thinking faded away, and gaiety and joy slowly came back.

After only three weeks, she would think she had been meditating for about five minutes, when it had actually been two hours. During this episode she seemed to free her mind or soul from her earthly body. She was coming to understand how Professor Dexter had gotten out of his body to meet her when she was in Saint Mary of the Plains College in Dodge City.

Bit by bit, Anna found peace in her life, and like the Korean priest, she found stronger energy given to her from the Holy Spirit. One evening, her father called and asked how it was with her Christian faith since she had become involved in meditation. Anna assured him that her faith had been strengthened beautifully and she felt closer to God than ever. However, her spirituality was not defined by any conventional church or religion. This would involve a different journey, unbeknownst to her at this time. She happily returned to her duties as a physician, believing that God wanted her to be of help to her patients. She was glad that she had found peace and became less concerned with life beyond.

7

Anna had little time to go deeper into meditation, partly because of her heavy workload at the hospital, and partly because of her family and children. She was content with the peace she had found after the many disturbances in her life. Then after about four months as a member of Art of Living, she was informed of a very important event, a meditation conference in Chicago at which a guru from India would talk about many interesting methods of meditation.

Eager for knowledge on the subject, Anna registered for a two-week, silent course in advanced meditation, though she did not know how much she would really learn. She attended the conference with the humble manner of a new member. Walking alone in the wide and long hallway leading to the conference room, Anna wondered if she would understand the guru from India. There were many people in the hallway and in the conference room. They were strangers coming from everywhere. Some seemed to be from other countries, because they were speaking some languages that Anna did not understand at all. Unlike other conferences Anna had attended, people attending this one were dressed very simply and generally spoke quietly.

Anna did not expect to know anyone. Her small body was lost in the line of people and unnoticed by passersby. As she stopped walking and stood aside to let people go ahead of her, she heard someone calling her from the direction of the conference room door: not loud, but in a voice clear enough for her to hear from more than fifty feet away. At first Anna thought somebody had called another lady with the same name as hers. She looked around and saw no one else who seemed to respond to the call. Then she heard her name again. Anna looked and saw a hand waving, beckoning her to come to the door. Anna saw the man who waved to her, a short, jovial, tanned person from India. She did not trust her eyes about the man who had called her, because she had never met him. She wondered who he was and proceeded to the door to meet him.

The man turned out to be Sri Sri Ravishanka, an Indian guru who had just come from Frankfurt, Germany, and was expected at the meditation conference. Anna was puzzled as to how he came to know her name and single her out of the melee of hundreds of people. Seemingly reading her mind, the smiling guru told her that he had known her for a very, very long time, though he had stayed as unknown to her. He knew she was coming and he stood at the door, waiting to greet her. He assured her that he was also aware of all her past problems and hard times. He asked her to see him later during the day for a message.

Anna was spellbound. She stayed silent, staring and smiling at him. For a moment, she thought the Indian guru had gotten information about her through the guide-teacher from Austin, but why? She was just an ordinary new student among thousands of members of Art of Living, and she resided in a place far away from India. Why did the guru wait to greet her at the door? From whom was the message? What was the message about? Anna was determined to see the guru.

During the session, the guru emphasized that meditation is not a religion. It is only the means for an individual to reach God, to feel the presence of God, and for God to speak. "We talk and think daily. When do we become silent to listen? We miss messages from God. It is only in silence that we can hear the voice of God. It is only in silence that you recognize we are one with God. You are a part of something magnificent. You are a part of something beyond yourself: this earth, this planet, this universe. You may not understand right away. But, the message will appear when you return to ordinary life. You will slowly understand."

For the whole day, Anna tried to look for him, but the guru was nowhere to be seen. She knew he would be consulting for different groups in many different rooms. She felt tired after several long sessions and came to the hotel lobby looking for a sofa in a far, quiet corner to rest awhile. When she found one, she saw him already there. Again, with a smiling face, he told her that he was waiting for her. The guru went straight into telling her the message that he assured her was from her master, whom he had contacted before he came to Chicago. Her master had been a physician and living in India more than four thousand years ago. He was very content with what she had been doing. He had also contributed intuition in many of her cases and would continue to do so for the better care of her patients.

Perhaps Anna would be introduced to her master on a day not far away. She would not have any major problems for the rest of her life; all were gone. The last thing she should know was that Omer was happy now and she should not worry about him. He was still with her and loved her.

The guru asked Anna to be alert for possible messages in the future that might not be coming from him but someone else.

It was a long message. That was why the guru could not tell her at the reception door. At the moment Anna was very sure that the guru had received information about her from Austin. However, when she checked later, her guide-teacher denied giving away anything about her to anyone.

Anna could not believe what she heard from the Indian guru. Was she so important an individual? No, she was only a humble, small lady who had been born in a Christian family in an undeveloped country and had drifted to the United States because of an unpopular and costly war. Her parents were only ordinary persons who had raised her after the codes of Confucianism and Catholic belief. She had reached her goal as a physician, and with the knowledge of a medical doctor she could not explain what was going on as so many things happened to her and around her. She was consumed by confusion, complexity, and even shame, not by pride or self-importance.

On the way home in the airplane in the clouds, Anna fell asleep and dreamed that she was flying by herself in another world, where all her departed patients had turned into angels and masters. They were looking at her from the clouds and waving to her.

CHAPTER 8
JOURNEY TO DESTINY

1

Anna had planned to increase her weekly meditation sessions upon returning to Austin, but the demands of her work did not permit her to do so. The reputation of her medical group had spread farther and farther. More hospitals in the area asked her to sign contracts to work with them, and the number of doctors in the group increased to more than fifty. Everything went smoothly and her mind seemed at peace. She continued her meditation work but only when she found time.

Meditation helped her accept her life as it was. The mysteries of birth and death no longer bothered her, nor was she as concerned about where the soul would go to after death. It was a privilege to come to this earth, she decided, and all come from God. The earth was a place to learn to improve and strengthen oneself by fulfilling one's duty and loving each other in order to come closer to eternity. What one believed does not matter as much as having a belief in God, she decided. It did not matter whether one believed in one Adam and one Eve; God may have created more than one Adam and Eve at the dawn of time. It did not matter how many days it took for God to finish his plan for the earth and his landscaping.

One thing was for sure: "He" had planned well and took care of all living things on earth. If God had planned carefully a place for all livings before birth, He was going to prepare a place for them to come after life on earth, Anna reasoned. Certainly would be a good place, a happy place. Most beliefs teach that we all come to God after death. Of course this was true. However, we are with God while living, too, because God is ubiquitous both in the visible and the invisible world. One should not worry about eternal confinement in hell, because like children, we all make mistakes. No father would send a son or daughter to the eternal fire. With all the things God does for human beings, he just needs one single commandment: love. It is not love for him, but for neighbors. He who did anything for a neighbor, did it for God. Anna believed there was no need for a long Holy Bible, Koran, Book of Mormon, Kabbala, or any other holy book. Only one word, "love," was enough, but it had to be the unconditional love that God requires from human beings, because they are a part of him.

A corollary of love was fulfillment, Anna thought. Each one on earth was assigned a task that needed to be fulfilled wholeheartedly. Gradually, Anna had come to see that Buddhism and Christianity were not very far apart. In Christianity, God is everything but also nothing at all. God is only the source of love. Buddhism does not talk about Divinity, but stresses compassion, benevolence, and above all, love, even toward animals. What one saw was just nothingness or illusion; what one perceived as existence was really nonexistence. A life span is just a tiny flash of time in comparison with eternity, but every soul must pass by this door, the earth, to come back to the source from which it came.

Each belief, though different in teaching, would end up back at the same source of love. One other strong belief of Anna's was that love caused God to give humans a life on earth. Life is a grace and goodwill from God, not an exile for humans and animals. By intuition, all species on earth tried to survive and take advantage of every second of their life and living source that God had prepared for them. God may not have created the first male and female as some religions believe; it may have come through evolutionary progress. Sperm and eggs of all species could have been the first work of God to bring life to the universe. It was the union of yin and yang that made life possible. Once setting us here, God wanted us to be happy and love one another.

There was nothing humans needed to worry about or fear when living under God's protection, Anna believed. He also needs each of us to care for each other, depending on the abilities that he endowed each of us with. That was our task on earth; that was how we related to each other. That was why she was glad to bring her two children into the world, as all parents are proud to contribute to the work of God in bringing their children to life and raising them up.

At the right moment, we would be called back. Anna accepted her fate as it had been and would be. Her knowledge of this life was too limited for her to understand the life beyond. Her purpose in life would be to learn, as much as she could. Each difficulty is a lesson. Omer's death and the pain given was another lesson. It was one that she passed with flying colors.

With her goals set and peace in her mind, Anna did not expect any favor or reward from her patients or from God. Though dedicated to her work, Anna was joyous once she had a weekend free. She had a beautiful plan for her and her children to enjoy during a couple of free days and felt completely happy with what fate rendered to her. She promised to accept without complaining whatever was to come.

Full of positive thoughts and acceptance, Anna enjoyed a beautiful Friday evening with her children until they were tired and went to sleep, leaving her alone downstairs. The whole house was very quiet and peaceful, and Anna felt somewhat lonely. She wanted to talk to somebody, but there was no one she could call at this hour of the night except God. She thought about praying before going to sleep. She had not been praying at night for a long time. When in the college dorm, she had kneeled to pray every night at her bedside before sleeping. She had forgone it since the beginning of her internship until now. She determined to resume her prayers as of this night. However, her praying would be different from her previous practice. She would not ask God for anything else but peace. She just wanted to talk to God; that was all. She sat on an armchair in front of a small altar and began her talk with God.

"Dear Lord. It's me, Anna. I know that you already know very well. I know that I don't know how to pray the right way, and no one taught me how, either. From now on, I would rather just converse with you.

"First of all, I know I have no control of either my birth or my death, so I do not know whether I have free will or if everything is predestined by you. I acknowledge that you have taken care of me well. From now on, I do not ask anything more from you but peace: just peace for my children and the rest of my life."

Anna went to work with very high spirits on Monday morning. Once sitting at the desk, she again buried her mind in the thick stack of files she was working on. Just then she was called to see a patient. She protested that there must be other doctors available, based on the schedule. She was told that the first assigned doctor was absent due to family problems, and the second one had a personal emergency. There was no alternative; Anna must see this patient regardless of all she had to do.

It turned out that the patient's name was Mr. Jerry Nicks, a white man of about fifty-five or so, who was admitted because of chest pain and heart problems. Anna walked in when Mr. Nicks was sitting on the bed looking at the door. He told her as she reached the bedside that he was waiting for her in this room and for this very moment.

Anna politely apologized to him for being late; she thought that he was angry and anxious to know his medical status after waiting a long time for a doctor. Mr. Nicks was silent during the course of the examination and paid no heed to what she was doing or saying. It surprised Anna that he appeared well, despite what was written on his chart. Watching the puzzlement on Anna's face, Mr. Nicks stared at her, looked her over from head to feet for a short time, then began to talk.

He said he knew what Anna was thinking, wondering why he was here in the hospital despite his mild condition. He told her that his purpose here in this room was to meet her. Hearing this, Anna thought that this man was bizarre, and she was about to walk away. Mr. Nicks raised his voice, saying that he was not crazy and imploring her to just listen to what he was about to say before she left.

He came here to give her a message, he said. The word "message" stopped Anna. She turned around and asked him to repeat what he just said. Again, Mr. Nicks said he came to the hospital not for his problem but to meet her and give her a message.

Immediately, Anna thought the message would come from Omer. She then asked him from whom the message came. Mr. Nicks did not answer her right away. He gently took her right hand in both of his, slowly opened her hand one finger at a time, and looked into her palm. Anna tried to pull her hand back, thinking that this man wanted to do a palm reading for her. Mr. Nicks said that he was not in professional palm reading for money, but occasionally he could do it when he received a message from above. He added that he would not leave the hospital until his message was delivered thoroughly.

Anna was in bad mood for being called and was about to walk away. But the word "message" suddenly reminded her of the meeting in Chicago where the Indian guru Sri Sri Ravishanka had mentioned to her the future message. Could this be the one the guru had talked about? She really wanted to know what it was about.

She turned to face Mr. Nicks in a position ready to listen to him, while Mr. Nicks still held her hand with both his hands. Mr. Nicks opened her hand and looked at her palm for a few seconds. He then released her hand and, after raising his eyes to her face for about fifteen seconds, he began to talk. "Dr. Vu, you do not need to know who I am. I am here as a messenger. I am asking you to have patience to listen to what I am going to tell you. It does not matter whether you believe what I am to say or not. I would just like to have my job done."

As he was saying this, Anna noted that some patients and a couple of nurses were standing around his bed to listen to him. He seemed not to care and kept speaking.

"There are two parts of the message. The first one relates to your troubled mind and the second is about your future. It was for confirmation that I looked at your hands and your face.

"As for the first part, I am going to bring you most of the answers to the questions that have troubled you. You should be happy that, one, the 'Above' has been very happy and content with what you have been doing and what you are planning to do.

"Two, you do not need to do anything for the entity from Above that human beings call God. And if you personify this entity to look at him as a man, then this man is very, very rich. He is a part of everything in this universe and many others. He is a part of you, and you are a part of him. He does not need anything from you. He does not need beautiful, big churches or temples, pagodas, or a mosque to live in. Do not try to imprison him in any worship place. He is ubiquitous in all universes. He has made the earth far more beautiful than anything people can build for him: flowers, plants, trees, music from the songs of birds, water from the sky and from streams, oceans, food from everywhere, light from the sun, moon, and stars, and electricity. And it is a privilege, a blessing, and favor to be here on earth. Think about the richest man of this world; what would he need from his sons or daughters? Since he owns everything, you should not worry about offering him anything, even your gratitude. He has no need for that.

"Three, do you know what the Absolute really wants from you? He does not need you to come to the church every day to bother him.

You should reserve time to do anything possible for your neighbors, for the hungry, for the needy. He needs you to care for the sick to fulfill your task on earth here in order to restore the power for your soul. There is no need to do this and that to thank him for bringing you into the midst of humanity, as most beliefs have asked their followers to do. It would be fine to do it, but it is unnecessary to a omnipotent God.

"Four, in terms of purpose here on this planet, you came to this place from your free choice. You had chosen to come here to learn. The earths are only places that souls can gain more knowledge to advance. The longer a life, the more knowledge it gains. That explains why life is very precious and why people try to cling to this earthly world.

"Five, you are here to potentially gain spiritual energy. Your personal effort determines how much you will gain in this lifetime. Once passing the line into another world, if you gain energy, your soul would transcend closer to God and be with others having the same level of energy. As for those who spend their whole lives cultivating valuable merits in monasteries or temples or doing charity works, they will become very powerful souls. They can perform healings with their power when requested, and we term it as a miracle.

"Six, doing charity work or favors for others gains five times the amount of spiritual energy being given away.

"Seven, saving a life gains the most, and destroying one causes the maximum loss.

"Eight, when you pray for someone, the line of energy will flow from you to him, and if you are powerful enough, the person in question can be healed; otherwise, there is not much effect. The more concentration there is on praying, the better the result. And the more people who are praying, the more power. Five times the energy flows from God to your soul compared to the amount of energy you send away in prayer.

"Nine, the last advice is that God desires for you to enjoy a happy and healthy life here on earth and not complain of having a short or long life span. You do not determine what standard to apply for 'short' or 'long.' Also, God is not preoccupied with setting up rules, laws, or regulations. These lead to worries and fear; fear and worries cause depression; sickness and bad health come from depression. God never makes people sick. Instead, they make themselves sick from too much drink and food, too much worry and fear. God has pity on the sick; that is why he sends them physicians.

"In terms of your future, as I said before, the Power above is proud of you and who you have become; you are going to have a very felicitous time. What you plan to do will be a great success and your career is not a thing to worry about. Money and wealth are your power for whatever you want to do in your future.

"One last thing: you will find love again and will be very happy.

"I may not ever see you again, and I am glad that everything will turn out beautifully for you. I wish you well."

On the way back to her office, Anna wondered whether she should pay heed to Mr. Nicks's message. Had he made the whole thing up or been sent by someone playing a joke on her?

She rejected that thought quickly. What would be his purpose in making up the whole thing? And no one could give him such a long philosophical message, just to tease her. He must have gotten the message from someone he really trusted. Or he might hear from

God, the way Ken Fulton, the Korean War vet, had related to her in the veterans hospital in Kansas City. Either this way or the other, he acquired the message, because Mr. Nicks was quite serious in his manner and confident in his delivery.

As for the first part of the message, most of what Mr. Nicks brought up agreed somehow with religions' teaching, such as God's gracious act in bringing a person to this earth and what one should do or avoid. All of these were specified in the Bible, the Koran, and every other religious code. However, there were some profound differences, too. In religions, one does good to be rewarded in heaven and avoids the bad to keep from being condemned to a burning hell, not to gain or lose energy before going into the afterlife. In religion, the purpose of life is to prepare the soul for eternal bliss, but in Mr. Nicks's message it was to amass energy in order to have a higher level of the soul in another world or to be closer to God. The most interesting part of the message had been the statement that "God needs nothing from us, even our gratitude." This sounded true to Anna, because she believed that everything we have belongs to God, anyway. The traditions of offerings and animal sacrifice could have been passed down from primitive worshippers who thought that offering a bribe was a way to please God. Mr. Nicks had strongly confirmed that his message was from "Above," meaning God. Now it was for Anna to judge whether she believed him or not.

As for the second part, the message said all good things about Anna's future. Everyone loves to listen to good things about their future, even from a palm reader, and Anna was no different. She really liked this part of the message, though she did not see how she could become rich and powerful. She was just an ordinary physician and also a single parent with two children to take care of.

Overall, Anna summed up the message by saying, "Above likes my work. I should perform as much good as I can to invest energy in my afterlife. I am going to have peace and happiness for the rest of my life."

Anna asked herself if this was the whole message. She found nothing special in it. As a physician, she had been trying her best to care for her patients, like any other doctor. She was also generous in charity, but within her financial means. She could not think of anything important she wished to do that would put her in need of a special message from heaven. There must be something hidden from her understanding.

And then she hit the jackpot. It dawned on her that the hidden things were right at the very beginning of the message: "What you are planning to do . . ."

She would write the story of her life. Living through so many circumstances, experiencing so many remarkable events, and searching so diligently for the answers to great matters like war and life beyond death, she had planned to write a book to record it all. She had been struggling to determine whether her life story should be made known to the public or not.

Part of her protested against the idea of making it public; after all, who would want to read about her personal matters? And even worse, what she thought of as interesting might be viewed as mere anecdotes by others. Furthermore, her experiences of the supernatural might be thought of as superstition, illusions, or worse, fabrication.

Finally, her reputation as one of the top physicians in the area could be brought into question.

However, the other part of her mind pushed her to go ahead and share with others her experiences, feelings, and wisdom on the mystery of life after death. This ambivalent attitude had been with her for a quite a while. Never before had she confided in anyone about her private life story, not to mention her plan to write a book about it.

But now she came to the conclusion that the message was telling her to go ahead and make her stories known to everyone. In disclosing her experiences, she had no intention of proving anything. She would simply register what she had seen, heard, or felt. What she experienced might give her a tiny hint of the road of the soul in life after death. What she had experienced could help others.

2

Making her life story known was not the top priority in Anna's life, however. The many twists and turns in her life had been enough; more than anything, she longed for peace, as the message had promised.

Days went by, and Anna tried to reclaim her daily life, focusing on children, friends, and career. The pain of her past was gradually subsiding, and she was determined to make the best of life by giving her attention to the important people and pursuits in her life. With her goals set, her life had become simplified: working, daily meditation, running for exercise, and taking care of her children.

Weeks and months passed. Life had become better for Anna, and she regained her usual gaiety. Perceiving this as an appropriate opportunity, many young men continued to show interest in her, but she would always quietly turn them away for the reason that she was too busy and not ready for a relationship at the time. It was not that her past still haunted her, but amazingly she considered all that had happened to her up to this point in life as "important lessons God wanted me to learn." Once in a while, Anna met one man or another, but these events never led anywhere, probably because she saw no immediate connection. Furthermore, after the intensity of her previous relationship, it would be difficult for her to meet anyone who could fill Omer's shoes.

As for the future, she believed intuitively that "what must come will come." She found strength in time spent with her friends.

During the time from Omer's passing until the fall of 2011, she would have every other weekend free to be with her girlfriends, as her kids were with their father. These were the people on whom Anna could always depend to look out for her benefit. They became her confidantes, her best of friends, her family. She felt she did not need any other relationship at this point. She had peace and love among friends.

One weekend evening in late July 2011, the group came over to Anna's house to enjoy each other's company, as they often did. They were all relaxing in her master bedroom, talking, enjoying some wine, looking through women's magazines, and surfing the Internet. After some intimate chatting, the group began asking Anna about her lifestyle, what attributes she would look for in a "perfect mate," her religious and political views, and so on.

The questions seemed relatively innocent at first, like those that might be asked in a typical online or magazine poll. But after the plethora of more personal questions coming at her, Anna began to inquire what the group was up to.

"Please don't kill us," one of them said. "We are going to open an online dating account for you on eHarmony, and we are paying for it."

At first Anna refused, but her friends implored her. After a long argument, at last, in order to make her friends happy, Anna conceded to let them open an account for her. But she told herself she had no plan to use the service. She thought, "Me? On a dating website? Nonsense! I am still attractive to many men and certainly don't need that."

The eHarmony website works by creating a person's profile based on personality questions and ultimately tries to match him or her with those of the opposite sex who have similar personalities and characteristics. They send the matched profiles to the email address of the person after those profiles are compared on levels of compatibility.

Anna's box blew up! She was receiving an average of ten male profiles a day! She was overwhelmed by it and she told her friend Letitia, "This is crazy and I am going to shut it down. I am not going to read all these lengthy profiles of men I don't know." All the while, she was receiving "icebreakers" from men interested in meeting her.

But her friends begged her to please just open one or two profiles and look at them, hoping that she would find someone interesting. Looking at the faces of her friends with their eyes full of love, compassion, and care, Anna finally said, "Okay, just one—not two—and then I will shut it down." She thought perhaps if she had just one date, this would be enough to appease her friends. Perhaps then they would leave her be.

For weeks she had been receiving anywhere from seven to ten profiles per day. But on this fateful day, there was only one—just one!

How odd was that for her? At break time on her rounds at the hospital, without any enthusiasm, she began to read the single profile, that of a man named David Wallace.

His profile caught her attention instantly, because what David had been experiencing in his life reflected her own story. It was almost like reading her own biography. He was a divorced father of two girls, had earned his master's degree, and enjoyed travel. His favorite destination happened to be Vietnam. That was quite a coincidence, Anna thought.

But what really attracted her to David's profile was the way he described his life up to that point. He, like Anna, was born and raised Catholic and had been married for just over nineteen years in what he termed as a "loveless marriage." He described sticking with his marital commitment for that long because of his children. He liked always to be there for them, emotionally and financially. But the comment that really connected with Anna was when David talked about setting aside personal happiness for those around him whom he was responsible for. She recalled that, for her, it was exactly the same situation.

For a while after reading David's profile, Anna sat in deep thought. His profile had moved her profoundly, and she was actually glad to have read it. Many questions came to her: What should she do? Should she wait and read some more profiles, or should she just stop reading? Was David the man for her life? Should she contact him right away? If yes, then how? She read the profile one more time and made the decision that David would be the person that fate had brought to her, and that she wanted to contact him, one way or the other.

Even though it was awkward and seemingly inappropriate for a woman to contact a man, especially given her culture and upbringing, she went ahead and sent an "icebreaker" to David. She thought it was a simple, easy, and less awkward way of connecting, using the site's email exchange.

Once having sent the email she was, like, as anxious and nervous as a teenager, waiting for the reply.

"Well, did he reply?" her girlfriends asked after just one day.

"Nothing yet."

For day two and day three, there was the same question and the same answer.

Then, just when Anna thought that David was not interested in her profile, he returned her "icebreaker." It was on Saturday, August 20. Immediately after that, the two had an email dialogue that lasted all Saturday afternoon. During that exchange, Anna recalled asking David if he was free for coffee on the next day, Sunday.

He told her, "I'm sorry but I already have a date. Not with another woman," he added, "but with my two daughters. I promised them a day at a water park on Sunday."

Anna was pleased that he had such dedication to his children, even more so that he would not break a commitment with them to meet a lady for the first time.

So, they both agreed to meet for coffee on Monday morning, August 22, at eight thirty a.m. It was easy to identify each other because they had a good idea of what the other looked like from the profile pictures. David arrived first and grabbed a table outside to wait.

As the moment of departure to meet David grew near, Anna

suddenly began to feel terrified. The thought of meeting a man that she only knew through Internet profiling made her tremble.

But she had an escape route planned. As a physician, it was fairly easy to instruct many nurses at the hospital to start paging her by nine a.m. She would only have to be with this man thirty minutes, and then she could flee the scene. She could then tell her girlfriends that she did give a try, but that it did not work out.

"I can do this," she told herself and headed to the coffee shop.

From the moment they met, there was instant connection. What started out as a short coffee date in the morning turned into three and a half hours of wonderful conversation! For both Anna and David, there was something "familiar" about each other. It was as if they had known each other before. The flow of their interaction was fun, loving, and natural. They talked seemingly about every topic and absolutely enjoyed each other during their meeting time. For them, there was an almost immediate sense of intimacy, of closeness, and of deep friendship. Each wanted to learn about each other, so the eagerness in the exchange was constantly present. They were careless about time and space around them. Anna's phone rang several times, but she seemed not to hear it.

As much as Anna was enjoying the conversation, she also felt a flux of emotion upon emotion stirring inside her. She perceived that getting to know David was in many ways like looking in a mirror: both were parents of two children, both were raised Catholic, both divorced, both endured the pain of a "loveless marriage." Sharing of all of these created a more intense connection for each of them. Neither was interested in a future relationship that would have no love or affection.

This coffee date was one of many millions in the history of mankind. But to David and Anna, this meeting had been an act of fate. The attraction, both physical and emotional, was instant. Both felt they had known each other previously, possibly in another lifetime. As they were leaving from their coffee date to go to work, David asked if he could see her again. She responded immediately that she would welcome that.

Upon arriving back at the hospital, Anna was bombarded by friends wanting to learn about the coffee date. She provided the details about David and the date for what seemed like a thousand times that day for those who cared for her. She told each one of them, "I think I am in love."

As she lay comfortably on her bed that evening, Anna remembered the details of the event of this surprising day in August. In her journal she wrote, "I met a man named David Wallace today. I think he is the one."

Unlike Anna, who had a tumultuous childhood beginning with leaving behind a war-torn country for good, David had had a typical northeast American upbringing. Overall, he had a very peaceful and delightful childhood, living his early years in a middle-class family with the Catholic influence of his parents and grandparents. David grew up in suburban Philadelphia, where one was either Catholic or Jewish. His family insisted on a parochial education in hopes of strengthening his faith in the Catholic Church.

From a young age, besides his curiosity about God and life after death, David had many questions on the role of the Church, on the Old Testament, and about sin. At eight years old, he asked the priest of his church about the differences between Catholics and Jews and what would happen to Jews when they died if they did not believe that Jesus was the Son of God. The priest looked at him almost patronizingly and said, "Son, just be happy you are with the chosen group of people." That answer only spurred more curiosity and spiritual confusion. All David knew was that the Catholic Church left him feeling empty and with no real relationship with God. To him, doing his "Catholic chores" brought no relevance, but he knew of nothing more significant elsewhere. He followed along, but all the while he felt lost and still longed for a real relationship with God.

David's peaceful existence came to an abrupt end the summer before his junior year in high school. At sixteen, he learned that his father was leaving home to be with a woman he had fallen in love with. No prior educational background had prepared him for the challenge that was ahead for him, his sister, his brother, and especially his mother. Many tears were shed and faces of uncertainty became the norm. The event was a colossal blow that caught David off guard, because unlike Anna, who had known turmoil since birth, this was David's first real experience with a tremendous life challenge. He could not really grasp what had happened, but the reality was that his dad had left home. It would take years, after David became a man, for him to understand what had happened and why. But he would come to understand that just because his dad left their home it didn't mean he'd left his life.

When David was trying to pull himself up from this blow, a second strong impact to his Catholic faith came during the time of separation and divorce of his parents. His mother, who did not ever want her marriage to dissolve, wanted to remain an active practicing Catholic. However, Catholic doctrine does not acknowledge divorce without annulment. His mother came to the parish priest to seek a pardon anyway. When she met the priest she indicated that she had never wanted to end the marriage. She had nothing to do with the divorce and she was so proud of her three children, all gifts of that union. The priest said that although he felt for her in her situation, unless she agreed to annul the marriage, she could no longer receive Holy Communion at Mass in church.

David's mother was devastated as her church, a lifelong place of solace, seemingly turned its back on her. This was a huge wound to his faith, too. Surely the God that he believed in would understand this situation and accept his mother regardless. The God that David hoped for was one who would be benevolent and compassionate to all, not exclusionary.

Years later, David realized that this significant circumstance would bring the addition of two new family members. His mother found love and joy again when she remarried, and David gained a tremendously loving and supportive stepfather. Through his father's relationship, he came to know and love his stepmother and recognized the deep love she had for him. From a perceived tragedy, something wonderful came: two more incredible human beings to love.

Despite these difficult early challenges, David stayed strong and fared well in school. After his last two years of high school, David was in the enviable position of being accepted to Clemson University in South Carolina. He would become the first college graduate in the immediate family. Clemson had a great reputation, but best of all, it was 750 miles away from home.

David's college years were among his favorite memories. He focused on his studies and developed lifelong friendships along the way. By chance, he met an old high school friend, Deborah, during the summer at home between his junior and senior years of college. They were happy to see each other again and seemed compatible. He recalled later that he could not have known her that well after several years of no communication whatsoever and during a long-distance relationship where he saw her only infrequently, given the distance between Philadelphia and Clemson, South Carolina. However, being convinced of his love for her, David moved in with Deborah when he graduated from Clemson in 1990 at the age of twenty-two.

Before long, the earlier romance of their relationship faded and daily life together became strained as conflicts arrived. David recalled that each time he tried to discuss relational problems with her, she would repeat that living together as adults took hard work and sacrifice and that David's image for their relationship was unrealistic and the fantasy of movies. Hoping the situation would change with time, they continued with an engagement and then married in April 1991.

Even though he wondered deep down about the unrest and conflicts he was having with her, and with lessons learned from the divorces of his and Deborah's parents, David proceeded on with the marriage, determined to make it work.

They stayed as husband and wife even though that deep connectedness that he yearned for was missing. He began to develop a career that would be, by American standards, successful. His position as a sales executive for a textbook-manufacturing company had proved a great vocation for David. He was young, intelligent, likable, and great around people. In other words, he was ideal for a sales career.

They made enough money, combined with her salary, to purchase a home in 1993. Later that year Erin was born. He kept doing well financially and could afford a bigger house in 1998. When Erin was four years old, Deborah became a stay-at-home mom. Having a nicer home and a beautiful car and growing successful by American standards, David still felt that something was painfully missing. As for his spiritual life, David no longer had any connection with the Catholic Church, even though he baptized his daughter as a Catholic.

David's troubles with his wife continued to mount, and discord at home became a permanent visitor. Their fights were loud and hurtful. David recalled not being confrontational as a young person, but that changed in his marriage. He could not rid himself of doubt, frustration, and a lack of intimacy.

Though living in a seemingly dysfunctional family, David still convinced himself that he could make this marriage work. He tried to assure himself of it countless times, but he knew that true and unconditional love for her was absent. In 2001, his daughter Shannon was born and also baptized Catholic.

Though David lacked religious conviction himself, he decided to baptize the girls Catholic and nurture their religious development up to the sacrament of First Holy Communion. After that, it would be by their choice. Confirmation is the time when young Catholics "confirm" their own Catholic faith, since they are then in a position to understand it more fully versus when they were infants and baptized by their parents' choice.

With one more family member, David became busier and by all accounts more successful by Western culture's standards. In 2003, his company was purchased by a larger firm with more national presence.

David wanted to pursue a new place to live, to give the family a fresh start, and pushed for a relocation to Austin in August 2004.

They moved to a brand new house in an affluent northwest Austin suburb. David put in a pool, bought a Mercedes, and joined a country club. However, the more material things he gathered, the more lost he became. Deep inside, he had originally hoped that by pulling his wife and children away from the "safety of the main family unit" in the Philadelphia area they would have no choice but to band together as a cohesive unit and become stronger.

In Austin, David graduated from Baylor's Executive MBA Program in May 2009 and became the director of the same program in fall of the same year. However, by the summer of 2010, David knew that not even these accomplishments could bring him the contentment he so deeply desired at home. Even a career change to something completely different could not hold back the rising tide of turmoil within his marriage and the discord of having no spirituality in his life.

He was certain by this time that he was not in love with his wife and that their volatile relationship was having a devastating impact on the girls. He wondered how much pain and soul-searching his father had gone through over his decision to pursue another road in his life years earlier. He asked his dad on several occasions, "How did you know it was time to leave?"

"Son, you'll just wake up one day and know," his father answered.

After another huge blowup with Deborah late one night, David took the dog and went walking for several hours; his heart pounded and his head hurt. He was lost and cried out to God for help. In what seemed liked an epiphany, he found a moment of clarity and knew what he was going to do.

He had given all he could for nineteen years to save his marriage. This long period of time seemed unfathomable, considering how unhappy and unfulfilled he had been. He did not realize how much a human being was capable of tolerating or rationalizing away. He could no longer ignore the fact that he had sacrificed so much for his family, but completely lost himself along the way.

In the fall of 2010, David and Deborah separated. She moved into an apartment, and their divorce was final in March 2011. As difficult as it was to see his kids less often, he knew at least there was peace in both homes.

Knowing that it was right, David set out to reclaim his life, and more importantly, himself again. He believed that an "indescribable and true love" was possible, as he had seen it expressed among some close friends over the years. Then he found it. On August 22, 2011, David met Anna for "just coffee" at eight thirty a.m. He knew from that moment that this woman would have the greatest impact on his life—he just had no idea how big and in how many ways.

3

As Anna left the coffee shop that morning, David asked to see her again. If their first date was a "coffee meeting," their second date was the "two-stepping" tactic, and it was a bold and daring move for David, who had never done that type of country dancing before. Anna did not expect that David would move so fast, but she agreed to the outing.

David was stunned with her charm and affectionate style. Once again, their conversation flowed easily, as with the previous coffee date. Anna remained charming as David acted the perfect gentleman. When they got back to Anna's home, she invited him in for a drink. They sat for a while on the couch and talked, and then they kissed gently for the first time.

Giddy with excitement, David left her home at two in the morning and he knew in his heart that Anna would be "the love of his lifetime."

As for Anna, when climbing into bed that night, physically tired but unable to sleep, she admitted that this date had been very significant, but at the same time she felt a great fear. She knew she had feelings and excitement for David, but somehow, she felt she was betraying Omer. She thought about running away from David as fast as she could. She even tried to convince herself not to see him again. She made up the excuse to her close friends that she disliked his shoes and perhaps should not see him anymore, but there was no denying their attraction to one another on the physical as well as the emotional level. Her friends told her to be brave and give him another chance.

What she did not know was that David was on much the same path she was.

Regardless of what was in their minds, they went ahead with the third date, and it was a playful one. They grabbed a quick lunch and went to a theater, neither for a matinee movie nor for watching a dumb flick, but for physical closeness: holding hands, whispering, and occasional electric kisses.

The following weekend, Anna invited David over for a dinner that would change her forever. She made him one of her favorite dishes. After cleaning up, they retired to the couch to cuddle. One of the things they did that evening was go through all fifty "personality questions" from the eHarmony site. It was amazing when they realized how much they shared, from relationship expectations to handling conflict and raising children.

Their affection grew into passion on the couch, and there was no doubt that their physical attraction had led them to the center stage. Anna and David were both nervous, because they knew where this was leading. Anna bravely invited David to her bedroom upstairs, where she passionately gave him everything for the first time. It was tender and scary at the same time. In tears, she told him that he had been her first and only one for a very long time. She was unsure of how she felt, though guilt was present for her because of what she saw as her betrayal of Omer by being in bed with another man.

David and Anna had gone through their share of adversity. Each had been trying to grip and hold on to someone, and both meant to hang on for a lifetime. Both had been badly hurt, and the fear of betrayal was combined with their determination not to end up the same way they had been. However, their physical, emotional, and spiritual attraction was so intense that it seemed as if they were meant to be together.

Through the fall of 2011, their relationship developed in a way that many others do as they continued seeing each other on a regular basis. After spending days or evenings with Anna, David always headed back to his house in Cedar Park. They wanted so badly to spend nights with each other, but they had to think, be careful, and set good examples for their children.

The holiday season was coming. Anna and her kids were to fly to Kansas for their annual get-together with their family that

December. Sadness overwhelmed the couple as they were temporarily away from each other, even though they had been together just over four months at this time. Once Anna was gone, David was quite melancholy and lonely. He stayed behind to have Christmas with his two daughters, but he missed Anna so. He knew very well that he would love Anna's family once he met them.

Before long, that opportunity came, in late January 2012. Anna took David to League City, Texas, to meet her parents. Although any gentleman planning to meet his girlfriend's parents would feel some trepidation, David did not. It seemed so natural for him to meet them and get to know them. He was fortunate enough to be familiar with Vietnam and its cultural side through his numerous trips there as part of the Baylor Executive MBA Program.

At the same time, David began staying overnight at Anna's house more often and eventually moved in by the end of January. His daughter, Shannon, who was with him half of each month, also began to stay over and became closer to Anna and her children, Emily and John. Erin, David's oldest daughter, came around more and opened up to Anna in a big way. A new family was forming, and it was apparent with each passing moment that this family was strongly enjoying a blessing from God.

Anna and David shared a tremendous relationship, filled with mutual respect, care, love, and affection. By any comparison, they had a life far better than most have the opportunity to share.

But still something was missing. . . .

David and Anna longed for a spiritual connection with God, something to give meaning to their life beyond being good children, parents, friends, or professionals. They both knew the Catholic Church and its patriarchal structure was not the answer for them.

They tried a couple of "seeker" churches that were Christian and nondenominational in nature. But they left each church service feeling that they still lacked the answer to spiritual connection in life.

One morning, David planned a breakfast with a former graduate-school classmate, Katie, who had just moved back to Austin from Colorado. This turned out to be anything but a casual coffee between two friends. During the course of their talk, David shared with Katie the joy of finding Anna and how much his life had wonderfully changed. He also explained further that even though he and Anna had a great relationship, they both felt a "disconnect" from the meaning of life and experienced no spiritual path. Katie talked of a small contemplative Christian community in Austin called the Church of Conscious Harmony. The name sounded a bit odd, but it seemed quite fitting to David. Katie explained, "The name Conscious Harmony is based on the fact that we live in a universe that is balanced and lawful. Consciousness of these laws and our relationship to Creation enables us to live in Harmony. Conscious Harmony means to align our life with God's purpose for human existence, to live a spiritually balanced, happy, and abundant life."

Katie also described the church as being one where everyone is part of "one human race," not separate individuals, religions, ethnicities, cultures, or nations. She suggested that Anna and David go with her the next Sunday to check it out.

They did and they were absolutely blown away. They walked out of the service on that fateful March day knowing that they had found a home at this church. Not only that, this Church community had also offered them the camaraderie and support to grow in spirituality with God. Their relationship with the new church went from spectacular to indescribable. They thought they had found connection to God and a plan to direct their intentional spiritual practice to the highest levels. Their personal bond also grew deeper from that moment on, and they did not want to be far away from each other, even for a single day.

In April, David had to leave Anna to take his students in the Baylor Executive MBA Program to Singapore and Chennai, India, for ten days. He noticed some trepidation in Anna on the day before his departure. At first, even Anna was not sure what caused her unsettled feelings, but the feelings remained. Then on the night before David left for Asia, as both of them sat enjoying a loving moment together, Anna realized that David was about to leave on a plane.

She finally knew what was making her uneasy. She could not escape anxiety and deep concern about David's departure, because it reminded her of the last time that Omer left her to head back to Belgium. Perceiving this, David was deeply moved. He tried to comfort her as much as he could by saying over and over to her that he was going to return just as soon as he could. He said it numerous times that night, trying to reassure her. But words would not ease her trepidation.

In addition to his verbal promise, he had to show her with actions. Time passed incredibly slowly for each of them during David's trip overseas. They talked frequently online, but their hearts ached and yearned for the other. They counted down the days until they would be in each other's arms.

The day of David's return finally came. It was on April 22, and the reunion was poignant. They held each other at the airport for what seemed like forever before going home. That evening was magical and neither doubted that they were soul mates. The level of their closeness gave them a sense that they had known each other beyond this lifetime. There was just no way they could be this connected, this inseparable. But they were.

Late that evening, while spending quiet time on the back porch, David, overcome with happiness and absolute love, asked Anna to be his wife. It was exactly eight months from their first date. "When you know, you know"—that was what they both said, and they did know, even from the first moment that they met. But David wanted Anna to know his level of commitment to her and their families. It was also their confirmation for life's journey and a spiritual path together. They began to plan for their wedding.

4

The wedding plans seemed effortless. It all just came together without any anxiety or hiccups. Through their many acquaintances, within days they had procured a minister, a photographer, a music DJ, and a venue for the ceremony and reception.

September 22 was the chosen day for the wedding, exactly thirteen months after their first date. Families and close friends all arrived a couple days before, and the weather in Austin that late September was glorious. As they liked to describe it, their wedding could not have come quickly enough. They realized that they loved each other as individuals and now they were about to become a couple. Their deep love was apparent to anyone they came into contact with. This final step for both of them would bring the most unexpected changes in their lives, since both had been hurt by previous relationships and the pain of loving can be too much at times.

For Anna, marriage had caused fear, and she thought she would never marry again. David had been hurt by the pain of a marriage that was challenged throughout, but he still had faith in the institution of marriage if he found the right woman.

The journey for them to come together had been so long, with so many unexpected curves, roadblocks, and cliffs. That day was truly the one that "the Lord had made" for them, and their love, led by God, would be the deepest that could be shared between two people. It would also have a tremendous impact on others. Their life together would have great meaning, if only to show to their children what a truly loving relationship could be between a man and a woman.

Knowing the significance and importance of this day, not only for themselves but also for their children, families, and closest friends, David and Anna thought that they must write their marriage vows to each other.

Anna was breathtakingly beautiful that day. She had a radiance that was apparent to all in the congregation. David was elegant, confident, assured, and about to become the happiest of all men.

As Anna approached the minister, she took David's hand. Both fathers had been asked to stand up for them because of the significance each dad had in them getting through life to this point. Their children also gathered around, and Reverend Kennedy began to speak.

When it was time for the vows, Anna went first. In an unexpected turn, she took the microphone and turned away from David to face the congregation. She said that she wanted everyone in attendance to know how much she loved them and thanked them for being there that day to witness a truly remarkable and unbelievable event for her.

She welled up with tears as she began. "My vows are a bit nontraditional in that I want to address our families and friends first.

"I made a date with a man named David Wallace on August 22, 2011, at eight thirty a.m. I only wanted to give this man thirty minutes. I told my friends to start paging me at nine a.m. that same morning because I was terrified and wanted a way out.

"I agreed to date after three years in hiatus only because of peer pressure. I wanted to run because of many reasons. I had been through a lot in the previous decade. It started with struggling to stay in a broken marriage for twelve years, and that finally ended badly seven years ago. Then I met this man who I thought I was to spend the rest of my life with; I thought God had given me a second chance at love after such a disastrous one. It, too, ended badly when he passed away in 2009. The pain left by Omer was in many ways so much worse than my divorce, because I had loved him intensely.

"I had viewed myself as a strong person, an immigrant. Like the rest of my family, I thought I had the strength of a horse. I found myself crippled with grief. My family stood by my side as I struggled for the next three years to redefine who I am and to just get my head above the water.

"The thought of falling in love and giving my heart to another person was intensely terrifying. It took a long time just to feel all right, to laugh again. I was content with my life, with my children, and a plethora of girlfriends, who were my rocks. I had ventured on a spiritual journey and thought that I was healed from the trauma... until August 22, when I met a man named David Wallace. There was a familiarity about David. It was as if I had known him for a thousand years. The thirty minutes turned into three hours and thirty minutes, and my phone was left silent as my friends continued to text and page me, thinking I needed rescue. My journey took on an entirely surprising twist and turn with David in my life. It was then that I realized my healing really began."

There was not a dry eye in the entire room. Anna put all the guests right inside her words. They could feel her for who she was, what she had been through, and the enormity of this second true love of a lifetime.

She turned to face David and spoke. "When I looked at you from the very beginning, it was like looking in the mirror: someone was just like me, in spirit, in thought, in words, in past mistakes, in our hopes for our children, in our hope for the future. I realized that we were now on the same path traveling from our own broken roads. These past months affirmed who you are and who we are together. I watched who you were when you were with me, with your children, with my children, with our children. You are the husband, friend, inspiration, and father that I have always dreamed of next to me. It feels as if we had been down this road together before, perhaps in a different lifetime; perhaps we've been given another chance to make it better this time. You are my healer, my teacher, my friend, and my love.

"Before my family and my friends and before God, I vow to walk the rest of this journey with you, body, mind, and spirit."

The room was completely silent as David embraced Anna as lovingly as he could and took the microphone. David also turned to face the congregation and took a moment to look around the room at his own family, his new family, and their dearest friends and was taken with absolute love and certainty as he began.

"As Anna explained so wonderfully, we did meet for 'just coffee' on Monday morning, August 22, 2011, at eight thirty a.m., and it was true that she was going to give our coffee thirty minutes, tops!

But those thirty minutes turned into three hours and thirty minutes. What I realized in that time together that morning was that there was something so incredibly comfortable and familiar about Anna. It was as if, as our wedding song suggested, we had known each other for a thousand years.

"My journey here today has also been a long one. I want to thank all of my dear family and closest friends who are here with us. You support me today as you always have. I am grateful to know you all are there any time I need you, and you know that I am here for you all, too.

"To Anna's family, I thank you for welcoming me and my children into your lives with open arms. You are all terrific and I look forward to many years to come as a member of that family and developing deep relationships with all of you. I am so humble that Anna's closest family and friends are all here in support of her in this incredible moment, just as you were when her road was dark. And to Anna's friends, you all are, and have always been, rocks for her. Thank you all so much for supporting Anna early in our time together when the thought of possibly loving again was so frightening. It is true that Anna, in trying to avoid having feelings for me, almost stopped seeing me after our second date—as she told her friends, 'I don't like David's shoes, and his shirttail is too long.' So thank you all for seeing that my intentions for Anna were pure and believing in me, too.

"This brings me to you, sweetheart. . . .

"Anna, in front of God, our children, our families, and closest friends, it is beyond words that I stand here today to commit my life to you. I have been blessed to be the one you have chosen to love with all that you have been through. That humbles me every day. The love

I have for you is truly a complete one of body, mind, and spirit. I have cherished every moment we have shared since we met.

"With you in my life, I am a better man, a better father, a better son, a better friend. I am absolutely better. I vow to be an even better husband to you. I would do anything for you, sweetheart, without hesitation or reservation.

"I vow to honor you above all and treat you with the highest level of respect and dignity as my beloved wife, my best friend, and my true companion, every day of our lives. I promise to be as healthy as I can be so that I am there for you and our kids permanently.

"I cherish this and every future moment we spend together and will bring happiness and peace to our life. Laughter will always be present. I will be an unconditionally loving and supportive partner to you and do my best every day to show you that you are the true love of my life.

"Please join me as we continue on this earthly journey together, hand in hand, all while growing together spiritually. You are the most beautiful woman in the world to me, both inside and out.

"I ask that you take my hand from this moment forward as my wife and make me the happiest man in the world! I love you with all my heart."

Then it was time, with vows declared, rings exchanged, and blessing made, for Anna and David to become husband and wife. But there was much more ahead for them. Through oceans, lands, wars, and dangers, they were guided by God to seek each other. It was God's will that they met in Austin to have an impact, to help heal others as they have been healed, and to show their endurance of incredible strife, pain, grief, prejudice, disrespect, anxiety, and fear, which they had faced head-on.

Recognizing that their bumpy roads brought them together, they realized that the goal is not to avoid the challenges in this thing called life, but to face them and keep conviction and faith. The paths they took to each other taught them lessons that they needed to learn; it was not a trial imposed by a resentful God.

In their living room is a plaque that says it all: "Life is not about waiting for the storm to pass. It's about learning to dance in the rain."

Those who know them believe that David and Anna were destined to meet each other. If there was ever any doubt that they were not hand selected by God to be together, consider this story:

In December 2010, a full eight months before ever meeting David, Anna was on a holiday shopping trip with friends to buy monogrammed coffee mugs for people she was working with. She had a long list of mugs to buy, each with the first initial of each recipient's last name on it. After completing the list, Anna picked up a mug with an initial W on it. Her friends kidded her, saying, "W? We don't need a W. No one has a W as a last-name initial!" For some unexplainable reason, Anna insisted on buying that large mug with the letter W on it. She placed it in her cupboard to hold baking items and then forgot all about it. At Christmastime in 2012, she pulled out her baking supplies to make some holiday treats and noticed the mug. She exclaimed with triumph as if to say, "David Wallace, you are sent by God to me! That is a glorious fact."

ACKNOWLEDGMENTS

Thanks from my heart to Mrs. Rose Bushman for her support, encouragement, and assistance when she was my colleague at Garden City High School in Garden City, Kansas. Without her, I might not have accomplished this book.

ABOUT THE AUTHOR

Trach Ba Vu was born in 1939 in a small village in North Vietnam at the onset of World War II. He grew up amidst constant wars of one kind or another.

At the age of sixteen, he and his family escaped from the socialist North to the Republic of South Vietnam, where he became a high school teacher. After two years as a teacher, he resigned to become an officer of the South Vietnamese Navy. Trach fought against the North the entire duration of the Vietnam War.

When the South Vietnamese government collapsed in 1975, he escaped at the very last moment with his family and immigrated to United States of America.

In the United States, he returned to school as a student and earned a bachelor of arts and a master's degree in mathematics. Afterward, he again taught high school mathematics, this time in a small western Kansas town.

Upon his retirement, he began to write this story. His writing reflects his experience with war and death and with the trials of immigration and starting a new life in the United States.

Quy Ngoai Church where Anna's grandfather's documents were hidden.

April, 1945. The Sunday school where approximately 1,000 children died of starvation after being abandoned by their parents.

1962. Trach Vu's first year at the Nha-Trang naval base.

The wedding of Trach Vu and Lan Nguyen on June 21, 1964.

Ha-Liuh Phuong Vu (Anna) at 1 year old in 1967.

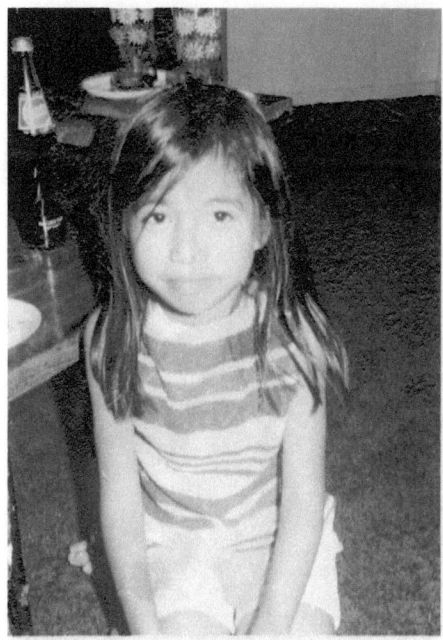

Ha-Liuh's (Anna's) first year in the US at 8 years old.

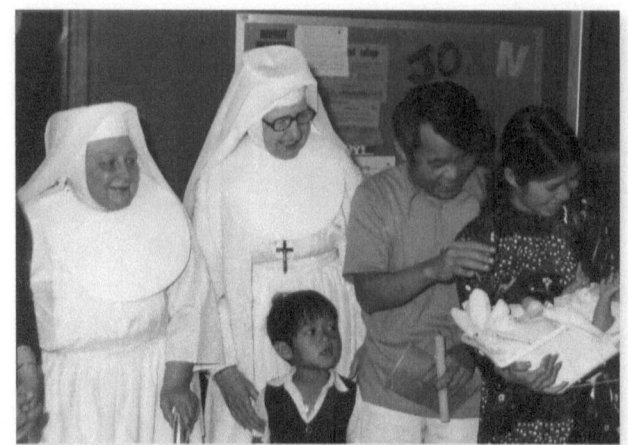

The baptism of Jerome Vu, the youngest child of the Vu family. He was the only child born in the US. His older brother, Triet, watches... accompanied by Sister Jerome and Mother Marianne.

Ha-Liuh (Anna), Linh, Gai Vu (Anna's Grandmother) and Triet at Jerome's baptism.

From left: Trien, Linh, Jerome, Ha-Liuh (Anna) and Triet Vu.

Anna Vu's medical school graduation in May 1994. (University of Kansas)

1998 Vu family portrait. (front row left to right: Anna, Trach, Lan and Linh Vu) (back row left to right: Jerome, Triet, Hoang Van (Anna's adopted brother and Trien Vu)

*Omer Verhaeghe
1964–2009*

*Hugo Verhaeghe:
Anna's patient
from Belgium,
2006*

*Omer and Anna,
2008*

June 2012. The "soon to be" new family. From left to right: Crystal (dog), David, Anna, John, Erin, Shannon, and Emily

September 22, 2012. Anna and David's wedding day in Austin, Texas.

November, 2012. Anna and David out dancing. Happy at last....

www.ingramcontent.com/pod-product-compliance
Lightning Source LLC
Chambersburg PA
CBHW020357080526
44584CB00014B/1065